the Bible
and the task of teaching

the Bible
and the task of teaching
by David I. Smith and John Shortt

The Stapleford Centre

The Stapleford Centre

The Old Lace Mill,
Frederick Road,
Stapleford,
Nottingham
NG9 8FN
UK

© The Stapleford Centre, 2002

First published 2002.

British Library Cataloguing in Publication Data
A catalogue record for this book is available from the British Library.

ISBN 1-902234-21-9

Set in 11/13 pt Goudy

Cover design by Hayman Graphics, Nottingham, UK.
Typeset at The Stapleford Centre, Nottingham, UK.
Printed by Progressive Printers, Nottingham, UK.

For Julia and Val

Contents

Preface

The Bible and education go back a long way together.

The Bible itself was formed in a process of handing essential stories and truths down across the generations. From New Testament times onwards, the spread of the Christian faith went hand in hand with educational activity. Prominent Christian thinkers such as Augustine, Comenius or Melanchthon contributed to a long and substantial tradition of Christian educational reflection, and in doing so helped to shape Western education.

Even today, when secular educational traditions have become more dominant in many contexts, Christian faith and education continue to interact. Apart from the education of adults and children that occurs each week in Christian churches, Christian education continues to be strongly represented in schools. The way in which it is represented differs in different national contexts. In some contexts, such as Norway, state education has an overtly Christian basis. In others the school system is more variegated – in the United Kingdom, for instance, around a third of state schools identify themselves as Christian. In still other places, such as the United States, Christian education finds its primary expression in networks of private schools and colleges. Moreover, in all of these contexts, interest in Christian education is not confined to Christian schools. Many believers who work in secular educational institutions also seek to reflect in a Christian manner on their work.[1] For very many people involved in education at all levels, the idea that education can or should be in some sense Christian continues to carry weight.

This book examines one particular part of what the notion of Christian education might mean. It focuses specifically on the ways in which the Bible might inform or guide educational reflection and practice. This is only a part, not the whole of Christian educational enquiry. However, given the central role which the Bible has always played in Christian thinking and living, clarifying the roles which the Bible might play in relation to education should be of concern to Christians teaching in all kinds of educational settings. This book is addressed to anyone, whether they teach in a Christian or a secular school or college or in another kind of educational setting, who would like to gain a broader grasp of how biblical faith can make a difference to the work of the teacher.

Rather than offer an abstract account of how the Bible *should* influence teaching, we have sought to identify the varied ways in which it actually *has* influenced teaching. In the following chapters we explore a diverse collection of examples of educational thought and practice. The purpose in doing so is to learn about the educational import of biblical faith by watching it in action in the thoughts and deeds of teachers and educational thinkers.

Although we discuss a range of particular educational ideas and practices, our concern in this book is not to develop or defend some particular set of proposals as the best or the only way to educate. Our main interest here is in the *process* which leads to them, in *how* they are arrived at. We are interested in how biblical faith has become interwoven with educational reflection, and how it might continue to do so. If we liken educational reflection in the light of scripture to painting a picture, our concern here is not to paint a single picture, but

---

1   See e.g. Cooling, 1994; Stronks & Stronks, 1999.

rather to ask what kinds of results are likely to be achieved by adopting various particular styles and techniques of painting. We hope to offer the reader a palette for his or her own use rather than a ready-framed work to hang up and admire.

A number of individuals and organisations have helped to make this project possible. The research leading to this book was based at The Stapleford Centre in Nottingham, UK, and was partly funded by the Bible Society's Research Grants Committee (formerly the London Bible House Research Fund). We are grateful to all our former colleagues at The Stapleford Centre and to Dr Martin Robinson and the members of the Bible Society Committee for all their support and encouragement. Many parts of the material have been incorporated into a MA module offered by the Institute of Christian Tertiary Education in Sydney, Australia; the work and feedback of the students who have taken this module over the last three years have helped us to clear up ambiguities and develop our ideas further. Parts of the manuscript have been presented at conferences and workshops in the UK, Canada and New Zealand, and feedback from participants has been useful. Wendy Booydegraaf, Jonathan Owens, Julia Smith, Joseph Stubenrauch and Rod Thompson read part or all of the manuscript and made valuable suggestions for its improvement. The remaining inadequacies remain, of course, our own responsibility.

David I. Smith and John Shortt

1

Human sacrifices and mad orchestras

The Christian Gospel came to Iceland in the tenth century. It immediately led to tensions between those who accepted the new religion and those who resisted it. Stephen Neill, in his history of Christian missions, relates a medieval story concerning the *Althing*, or great gathering of local assemblies, of the year 1004:

> The heathen men summoned a great gathering, and there they agreed to sacrifice two men out of each quarter and call upon the heathen gods that they would not suffer Christendom to spread over the land. But Hialte and Gizor had another meeting of Christian men, and agreed that they too would have human sacrifices as many as the heathen. They spoke thus: "The heathen sacrifice the worst men and cast them over the rocks or cliffs, but we

will choose the best of men and call it a gift of victory to
our Lord Jesus Christ, and we will bind ourselves to live
better and more sinlessly than before, and Gizor and I will
offer ourselves as the gift of victory of our Quarter."[1]

Clearly, the Christian leaders portrayed in this story were determined not to be outdone by their heathen counterparts. "Whatever
the heathen do, we Christians will do it better," is the spirit of their
response. If they offer human sacrifices, then we will offer them too,
just as many as they offer. If they offer the worst men, then we will sur-
pass them and offer our best men. In doing so we will be offering a gift
of victory to Christ.

However, this impulse towards excellence is not all that is going
on. If it were, the results would be grotesque – *Christians* excelling by
offering human sacrifices? Hialte and Gizor do not only promise to
excel; they change the terms on which excellence will be measured.
The heathen sacrifice by throwing folk off cliffs, but *we* will sacrifice by
binding ourselves to live more sinlessly. The heathen offer third-rate
deaths, but *we* will offer consecrated lives.

In order to excel in a Christian manner, Hialte and Gizor carry out
a daring redefinition of the cultural practice concerned. This redefinition is enabled by the language of the New Testament, which offers
the paradoxical image of *living* sacrifices, offered continually to God.[2]
This is the kind that the Christians will offer. Without this radical
change in the meaning of human sacrifice, they would have found
themselves achieving excellence at the wrong thing. They would
have been just as good as the heathen at something that should not be
happening at all.

Whether or not it is strictly factual, this story reflects in a clear and
economical manner an often repeated pattern. The Gospel arrives,
and a cultural practice is redefined in a far-reaching way under the
influence of the Bible. Such transformations have happened in many
times and places over the past two millennia.[3] Offering sacrifices
seems a relatively straightforward cultural practice, yet we see it

---

1   Neill, 1986:91-2.
2   Cf. Romans 12:1: "… offer your bodies as living sacrifices, holy and
     pleasing to God …".
3   See e.g. Wessels, 1994.

turned inside out in the light of Christian faith. We might then reasonably expect Christians to look for far-reaching changes in a cultural practice as complex and as closely bound up with our basic values and aspirations as education.

The Bible and Christian education

We would be justified in such an expectation. Believers have repeatedly advanced the claim that Christian education should not simply be regular education done better, but rather education reworked on a Christian basis. Such claims reflect a desire not to be caught up in the pursuit of an unexamined excellence. Instead, there is a desire to know whether we are pursuing the right project in the first place, to know what particular kind of excellence will really channel grace, life and peace.

The Bible has a role to play in this rethinking process, just as it did in our Icelandic tale. While they may have varied ideas about the precise role of the Bible in the Christian life, Christians of all confessional backgrounds regard the Bible as in some way authoritative. Talk of Christian education must therefore mean, among other things, education which is in some way influenced or guided by the Bible. If we turn to published Christian discussion of education it is not hard to find statements such as the following:

> A Christian worldview takes as its starting point that the Bible is God's authoritative Word for life. Scripture is God's inspired self-disclosure that calls for obedience and response ... If the Bible is relevant for all of life, then it is also relevant for education.[4]

> Christian educators must carefully examine the biblical foundations for Christian education. Scripture is the essential source for understanding Christian distinctives in education.[5]

---

4   Van Brummelen, 1994:25.

5   Pazmiño, 1997:17.

There is, then, nothing new in the claim that Christian education should be in some sense biblically informed. Such claims are fairly commonplace among Christian educators. In a sense, however, the really interesting questions begin once we ask how the claim can be translated into practice. There doesn't seem to be anything too problematic or puzzling about the idea that a *doctrine* could be biblical. But the Bible seems to have little directly to say about education, and does not even mention schooling. What does it actually mean in practice to say that it is a 'foundation' or a 'source' or 'authoritative' for education? In what sense could a modern school administration or a chemistry lesson or a theory of language learning be 'biblical'? What kind of connection could there be between the Bible and the bulk of present-day educational concerns?

Lack of clarity at this point is a source of bewilderment among both Christian and non-Christian educators. Many Christian educators would like to believe that the Bible could speak to their educational efforts, but find it hard to see what this would mean in practice. Others find an outlet for their desire to affirm the Bible's authority in what can sometimes seem highly arbitrary insertions of biblical texts into teaching materials. Teachers in Christian schools with whom we have discussed these issues have reported (with amusement) instances of references to the fire of God being brought into work on temperature and Jesus' reference to Peter as a rock being inserted into the study of geology. In neither case does there seem to be much real connection between the educational topic and the concerns of the biblical text. The process involved is more one of vague word association than the transforming power of the Bible. In the face of such practices, non-Christian educators have wondered aloud whether the idea of Christian education has any genuine substance.

Both the uncertainty of some and the over-enthusiasm of others fuel a third attitude, one of scepticism that the Bible can be defensibly related to education at all. Appeals to the Bible, some would argue, are just a tactic that Christians use to make themselves feel more righteous and secure while they actually carry out the business of education in much the same way as everyone else. Is such scepticism justified? Answering that question is a central concern of this book.

How is the Bible authoritative?

In a poem titled *the fanatical orchestra*, Austrian poet Ernst Jandl describes a beleaguered conductor facing an orchestra whose performance is bizarre in the extreme.[6]

the conductor raises his baton
the orchestra brandish their instruments

the conductor opens his lips
the orchestra strikes up a howl of rage

the conductor taps with his baton
the orchestra pound their instruments to pieces

the conductor spreads out his arms
the orchestra flutters around the room

the conductor lowers his head
the orchestra burrows in the ground

the conductor sweats
the orchestra battles with raging torrents of water

the conductor looks up
the orchestra races towards heaven

the conductor stands aflame
the orchestra collapses in an ardent blaze

At first glance the musicians' behavior seems wild, out of control, beyond any rhyme or reason. However, as the poem progresses it soon becomes clear that their madness is not arbitrary. As the poem's title indicates, they are in fact fanatically trying to obey. Every slight gesture from the conductor brings forth actions from the orchestra that correspond to it in some way. This is no rebellious anarchy – the

---

6   'das fanatische orchester' (Jandl, 1981:60). The following translation is ours.

musicians have the highest regard for the conductor's authority. What they lack is any sense of how to obey *appropriately*, any discernment regarding which of the conductor's motions are really significant. The image of the conductor with outstretched arms and sinking head at the heart of the poem recalls the image of Christ on the cross, and suggests that the sometimes curious attempts of believers to obey their Lord are not far from Jandl's mind.

Jandl's musicians do not need convincing of the conductor's authority, yet their attempts to obey are bizarre; they lack wisdom concerning *how* the conductor's authority actually operates. This is precisely the question at the heart of this book: *how* is the Bible authoritative for education? How does its authority actually operate? As Jandl's poem illustrates, this is different from the commonly debated issue of the basis of biblical authority. The underlying questions in debates over the inerrancy or infallibility of the Bible are: wherein lies the authority of scripture?[7] Why should we regard it as authoritative? The trouble is, the most conservative believer could in principle believe the entire contents of the Bible to be inerrantly true, but still have very little idea of how their authority could be applied to a particular educational situation. Proclaiming the authority of the Bible does not in itself tell us how to obey it.

A provocative recent attempt to rethink the idea of biblical authority in this vein can be found in an article by N. T. Wright, titled 'How can the Bible be authoritative?'[8] Wright suggests that many previous discussions have simply assumed that we already know what authority is and have then gone on to look at how the Bible carries such authority. This, he argues, has had two undesirable consequences.

First, we end up applying inappropriate models to the Bible. For instance, we approach a text that is in large measure made up of narrative and poetry in the light of an idea of authority which is associated with the workings of a rule book or a set of instructions. We therefore focus our attention too selectively on particular commands or timeless truths, failing to ask in what manner a *story* could be authoritative. As

---

7   Inerrancy is the view that the Bible contains no errors, infallibility allows for more imprecision in incidental details. Both stand at the more conservative end of the theological spectrum and contrast with views which compare the inspired quality of scripture with that of great literature.

8   Wright, 1991.

Wright puts it, "it is one thing to go to your commanding officer first thing in the morning and have a string of commands barked at you. But what would you do if, instead, he began 'Once upon a time...'?".[9] The Bible is not just made up of commands or instructions – so in what other ways is its authority expressed?

A second consequence, Wright argues, is that the authority of the Bible gets misused as a way of dominating people and putting them into little boxes. Appeals to the Bible can become a way not of injecting new life but rather of silencing further discussion. Claims that a particular educational practice is 'biblical' can function as a way of insulating it from criticism, suggesting that it is uniquely and comprehensively approved by God and therefore must be accepted without question as the right thing to do. Instead of opening up new avenues to explore, this kind of appeal to the Bible can seem to suggest that there is really nothing more to discuss.[10]

Before wielding the Bible as a form of crowd control, we should, Wright suggests, be first asking what God's authority is like and how God exercises authority "to liberate human beings, to judge and condemn evil and sin in the world in order to set people free to be fully human".[11] On this view, biblical authority should not be used to manipulate and control but should rather bring new life, liberating us from the fetters of our foolishnesses and idolatries.

Both of Wright's concerns are relevant to our question concerning how the Bible relates to education. We can phrase his concerns as two further questions. Firstly, how should we respond in educational terms to an authoritative text which is made up not just (or even primarily) of instructions or principles, but also of narratives, poems, laments, and the like? What aspects of the Bible should we be attending to? Secondly, how can the Bible be brought to bear upon education in ways which are life-giving, which open up fruitful avenues to explore rather than prematurely nailing everything down and ending discussion?

---

9   Wright, 1991:10.

10   For a description of a stark example of this practice, see Smith & Carvill, 2000:153-154.

11   Wright, 1991:16.

Changing times, changing contexts

The Bible and education go back a long way together, but there are good reasons to give fresh attention to their interrelationship at this particular point in time. The latter half of the twentieth century saw a modest renewal of scholarly interest in the relationship between Christian faith and education. This was reflected not only in the publication of books and articles, but also in the appearance of new journals devoted to discussion of Christian education.[12]

At the same time the wider cultural context continues to develop and change. The trust in objective reason, scientific investigation and technological innovation to light the way ahead which has played such a major role in modern Western culture no longer seems as self-evident or self-assured as it once did. Many have questioned these emphases and pointed to the rise of a 'postmodern' culture in which nothing is certain and life is more complicated that it once seemed.[13] This, together with an increased awareness of the role of diverse commitments in educational debate has begun to shift the ground under discussions of Christian education.

Two changes are particularly relevant for present purposes. First, the idea that science and reason will deliver a single, impartial, true

---

12   For instance the *Journal of Christian Education* in Australia, the *International Journal of Education and Religion* in Britain, the *Journal of Education and Christian Belief* in Britain and the United States, and, also in the US the *Journal of Research on Christian Education* and *Research on Christian Higher Education*.

13   See e.g. Middleton & Walsh, 1995. In the field of educational philosophy, consider, for instance, the influential philosopher of education Paul H. Hirst. In the 1970s, his influential writings sought "a form of education knowing no limits other than those necessarily imposed by the nature of rational knowledge and thereby itself developing in man the final court of appeal in all human affairs" (Hirst, 1974:43). More recently, however, Hirst has criticised the "hard rationalism" on which his earlier work was based, now arguing that reason is "exercised from the very start in inextricable involvement in our exerting our other given capacities" (Hirst, 1993:184). Might these include faith? We will discuss Hirst's views concerning Christian education in chapter 2.

picture of the world has been under sustained pressure. Arrayed against it are a variety of particular perspectives jostling for position. While this has made claims to truth more problematic, it has also created new spaces for exploring ways in which the Bible might inform education. If educational inquiry is understood as requiring a neutral starting point, a voice speaking from nowhere in particular, any substantial role for biblically oriented reflection seems excluded in principle. Once the role of particular perspectives and commitments is recognised as unavoidable, the possibility that the Bible might have something to say at least becomes more conceivable.[14]

Second, if educational thinking is understood largely in terms of logical relationships between propositions, attempts to show how the Bible is relevant must work within fairly narrow parameters. The focus of attention will be upon whether the Bible provides us with a set of basic propositions from which educational consequences can be logically deduced. The debate, as we shall see in the next chapter, then tends to revolve around whether this can be done.

Recent developments in both educational and theological discussions point to additional possibilities. Both educators and biblical scholars have, for instance, rediscovered and explored the importance of narrative for our understanding of ourselves and our world.[15] Much of our everyday understanding takes the form of stories rather than concepts. Which happens if we take the Bible's character as narrative seriously, rather than immediately translating story into doctrine? What stories shape our lives and lie embedded, whether explicitly or implicitly, in our school curricula?

Similarly, metaphors are now no longer viewed as a mere poetic decoration best replaced by literal speech, but rather as something which colours much, if not all, of our thinking and acting.[16] We think in and through images: the bloom of youth, the ship of state, the path of life. Are the metaphors in scripture mere decoration best reworked in more prosaic language, or are they important vehicles for truth in their own right? And what of educational metaphors? Seeing a school as a factory or a garden can lead to very different patterns of practice. Could biblical imagery be relevant?

---

14   For further discussion on this point, see Wolterstorff, 1997, 1999.
15   See e.g. Egan, 1988; Fackre, 1983.
16   See e.g. Ortony, 1993; Soskice, 1985.

There have also been reactions against the kind of scientific dis-section of the Bible characteristic of historical criticism, which tended to focus on questions of when the text was written, how it was com-posed and what really happened behind the text. One such reaction, which has given rise to explicitly educational reflection, can be found in the movement known as canonical criticism.[17] The interest here is in how the biblical text was passed on through the generations and on whether its final shape has anything to teach us about what we should pass on to the next generation.

Such developments have broadened the context within which questions about the Bible and education must be debated. We are not suggesting that they should be uncritically embraced, but rather pointing out that they have opened up new avenues for investigation. Our reasons for focusing afresh on the relationship between the Bible and education do not, therefore, arise only from the sense of existing confusion and lack of clarity. We also believe that significant resources for understanding the relationship remain under-explored by many practising Christian educators, let alone their critics. The chapters which follow attempt to chart some of the promises and perils of exploring such resources.

The road ahead

We will examine in turn a range of possible approaches to relating the Bible to education. We will consider the strengths and weaknesses of approaches which focus on:

- the educator's personal qualities as they are shaped by the Bible (chapters 3-4);

- what the Bible teaches about the world and its relationship to education (chapters 4-5);

- the narratives which can be found in both scripture and education (chapters 6-8);

---

17   See e.g. Brueggemann, 1982; Sanders, 1984.

- the role of metaphor in the Bible and in education (chapters 9-11); and

- the educational models presented in both the content and shape of the Bible (chapters 12-13).

As we have explored these approaches we have become increasingly convinced that they should not be seen as alternatives, or even placed in a hierarchy of importance. We see them more as different strands of a rope. While we have unpicked the strands somewhat in order to look at them more closely, they belong together, intertwined. Together they form something more substantial than any of them taken individually. We will return to this point at the end of the book.

Before beginning to examine the rope, one more task is essential, and this is taking a longer, harder look at the skepticism described above. Various cogent objections have been made to the very project of relating the Bible to education. These not only deserve to be given careful attention as thoughtful responses to the question at issue, they can also help us to gain a clearer sense of how the land lies, of where the difficulties and possibilities are to be found. Examining these objections is the task of chapter 2.

2

The case for the prosecution

To many Christian teachers the puzzling point may not be the idea
that the Bible has something to say to educators, but rather the idea
that there is a problem with this. The Bible is, after all, "God-breathed
and ... useful for teaching, rebuking, correcting and training in righ-
teousness," so that we might be "thoroughly equipped for every good
work."[1] What's the problem?

There are, in fact, a variety of problems. We do believe that the
Bible can speak in life-giving ways to present-day education, but this
does not mean that the problems can be lightly dismissed. They have
been noted by both Christian and non-Christian educators; some
have gone so far as to argue that there is no rope connecting the Bible
to education, only a few frayed ends. Whatever our ultimate conclusions, there are good Christian grounds for welcoming critiques which

---

1   2 Timothy 3:16-17.

might promote sober self-examination. We propose, therefore, to take a good look at a range of criticisms in this chapter before moving on to a positive response.

Christian education as a form of nonsense

A short article by the prominent educational philosopher Paul Hirst, first published in 1971, still offers a good place to start, since it deals clearly and succinctly with a number of important issues.[2] Hirst argued that Christian belief should not and cannot serve as a legitimate basis for educational reflection. In fact, the whole quest for a Christian approach to education should, he claimed, be regarded as "a kind of nonsense ... just as much a mistake as the idea that there is a distinctively Christian form of mathematics".[3]

Part of Hirst's argument was that educational thinking should be based on objective reason, and so Christian beliefs can at best add their vote of confidence to positions already established on independent rational grounds.[4] In other words, we *should not* try to think constructively about education on the basis of Christian belief. This aspect of Hirst's argument has become dated over the intervening years; Christian writers have not been convinced, and Hirst's own view of reason has shifted.[5] Of more enduring interest is another strand of his argument, which claims that even if we wanted to develop a Christian form of education, it *cannot* be done.

Hirst suggested that even if Christian education is seen as desirable, it is in practice impossible to define its nature. He argued that Christians are faced with a dilemma. On the one hand, they look at what the Bible says specifically about education, but find that it is far from easy to make the application to education in our different historical and cultural context. On the other, they find themselves deriving general moral principles from Scripture which are too broad to determine any specific educational consequences. We will expand on

---

2   Hirst, 1971.

3   Hirst, 1971:305. On the question of whether there is a Christian perspective on mathematics see recently Howell & Bradley, 2001.

4   See also Hirst, 1976.

5   See Hirst, 1993; Thiessen, 1990 and chapter 1, note 13.

each of these points, and supplement Hirst's argument with some examples.

In search of specifics

If we want to teach in a way that is faithful to the Bible, an obvious first step is to look closely at what the Bible says about education. Here, however, Hirst saw difficulties.[6]

The first problem we find is that the Bible does not in fact have much to say about many present day educational practices and concerns. Look in a biblical concordance and you will not find entries under headings such as examinations, teaching methods, truancy, or even schools. This seems to limit what can be argued directly or conclusively from the biblical text. Consider the following range of arguments, all of which have been put forward on the basis of the Bible:[7]

1. The Bible does not mention schools, but places educational responsibility in the hands of parents. Christians should therefore reject the schooling paradigm and turn to home education instead. It is parents who are called and authorised to educate children, and it is not the place of the state or the school to usurp this role.

2. The Bible does not mention schools because the school institution as we know it did not exist in its day and culture. As time has passed, and industrialisation has progressed, the amount of specialist knowledge which children must acquire has increased dramatically. Our situation is therefore quite different from that of ancient Israel. Schools are now necessary. We should continue to heed the biblical injunctions for parents to nurture their children in faith and godly conduct, while accepting that other aspects of education need to be undertaken in schools by specialists, who need not be Christians.

---

6   Hirst, 1971:306.

7   Adapted from Weeks, 1988:3-5.

3. The situation has changed as described in 2 above, but we should look for the underlying educational principles in the biblical passages addressed to parents and apply these to new forms of teaching and learning such as schooling. Schools as we know them were not around then, but if they had been, the same principles would have applied. Schooling is now needed, but it should be Christian schooling, biblically grounded and carried out by Christian teachers as an extension of the parental task.

4. There were village schools, synagogue schools and pagan schools in New Testament times, and there are no instructions in the New Testament for Christian parents to withdraw their children from such schools. We must therefore assume that the children of converted parents continued to attend them, and that this was not considered a problem by the believing community. This suggests that we would be justified in adopting the same attitude towards today's secular schools.

Our present concern is not to decide which of these arguments is right. The issue at stake is the fact that all of the arguments claim consistency with the Bible, and that it is not easy to see how the Bible could be used to decide conclusively between them.[8]

This example highlights the difficulties involved in arguing from silence. What if we focus on those aspects of education which the Bible does deal with, such as the teacher-learner relationship? This may get us further, but it will not, Hirst argues, remove the historical and cultural gap between our educational setting and that portrayed in the Bible. We cannot simply transfer practices from the Bible to the present day. Should biblical Christian educators (Hirst might have

---

8   Weeks (1988:4), who only lists arguments 2-4, suggests that Deuteronomy 6, with its concern that the whole life of the child be surrounded with the truth that springs from God's revelation, decides the issue in favour of argument 3 above. It seems, however, to be equally compatible with 1 (which Weeks does not list), and it is at least open to debate whether it is not compatible with 2 and 4 given a strong Christian home context. See further Hill, 1978; Weeks, 1980.

asked) wear sandals and teach on mountainsides, or teach learners in groups of twelve?

To get round this difficulty, Hirst argues, Christians end up trying to abstract more general biblical principles from the cultural particularities of the text. This leads to endless debates over interpretation. Christians continue to disagree over which principles should be derived from the biblical text and over how they should be applied in the present-day situation. If the Bible leads so many different Christians to different conclusions, must we not suspect that it is not really the Bible that is the determining factor?

Problems with principles

There is, Hirst argues, a further problem with general principles derived from Scripture: they are not sufficient to yield any specific educational recommendations. Consider an example which may help to illustrate Hirst's point. Suppose a Christian school declares its commitment to the principle that each individual child should be loved and affirmed since he or she is made in God's image. Such affirmations are common in Christian school mission statements. Suppose also that this school is engaged in reflection on its assessment practices. It is not too hard to imagine the following arguments being pursued:

1. One problem with exam grades is that the exams tend to take over the whole process of teaching and learning. Pupils soon work out that what is really important is what's on the test. Some of our wider educational goals get pushed into the background, or even undermined, as we become fixated on what can be tested in an exam. The need to cover the exam syllabus and to push pupils towards better grades leads to time pressure, which prevents teachers and learners from exploring points of interest further. Valuable learning time is spent on exam coaching. And why do we put up with this? Exam grades are mainly for apple-sorting; they are there so that society can decide who to put in which jobs rather than for any genuinely educational reasons. The grading system places pupils under stress, and tends to favour pupils

with certain kinds of gifts. Those who are not good at writing exam answers get labelled as failures, whatever other talents they might have. If we really love the children and see them as made in God's image we should not follow secular education – we should be radical and do away with grades.[9]

2. Grading on the basis of exams may have its weaknesses, but it does give an indication of who has done the work and of what their aptitude for it might be. If pupils leave school without the grades and qualifications which our society requires, employers and colleges will not take them seriously. They may not be able to get into the field to which they feel called – how could it be loving to leave them unequipped for the society in which they will have to live and serve? If we love the children in our care we will provide them with the opportunity to earn the certification that they need to flourish in this society.

Once again, the point here is not whether these arguments are right or wrong, but rather the role played in their construction by the biblical principle. There seem to be two problems. The first is that the biblical principle does not in itself tell us what to do. In order to have this kind of discussion we need to draw upon our experience of pupils and exams, on psychological ideas about the kinds of duress which children might suffer, on ideas about the society in which they live, on theories of exam-based assessment and what it can or can't show, and so on. It seems to be these varied sources that provide the grist for the argument. The biblical principle looks as if it might be more like the finishing touch than the foundation.

This leads to the second problem, which is that the principle seems compatible with opposite courses of action, in this case keeping exams or abolishing them. It does not determine the decision one way or the other. If a biblical principle can point in two opposite directions, then how can it be maintained that the Bible has any distinctive contribution to make to education?

---

9   For a version of this argument put forward in connection with a "design for a biblical Christian school", see Adams, 1982: 115-124.

All of this leads to the suspicion that appeals to biblical principles might be little more than a rhetorical overlay, taking decisions arrived at on other grounds and lending them an aura of divine authority. This suspicion was voiced in vigorous terms (in a publication which appeared the same year as Hirst's article) by Alasdair MacIntyre:

> Injunctions to repent, to be responsible, even to be generous, do not actually tell us what to *do* ... Christians behave like everyone else but use a different vocabulary in characterising their behavior, and so conceal their lack of distinctiveness ... All those in our society who self-consciously embrace beliefs which appear to confer importance and righteousness upon the holder become involved in the same strategies. The fact that their beliefs make so little difference either to them or to others leads to the same concern with being right-minded rather than effective.[10]

The charge is that Christian rhetoric is used not because it adds any substance to our educational ideas, but merely because it makes them seem more important and makes us feel that we must be in the right. Such accusations, even if they are far from the last word, ought at least to lead Christian educators to some serious self-examination.

Misreading the Bible?

Hirst's misgivings emerged from reflection on the nature of education. A further set of misgivings emerge from reflection on the nature of the Bible. Perhaps the Bible is simply not intended to tell us how to carry out education. If so, then it would be no mark of disrespect for the Bible if we left it out of consideration in educational discussion, any more than it would be a sign of flouting the highway code if we did not consult it when baking cakes. To read the Bible as offering educational recommendations may be to misread it.

Examples of such misapplication of the Bible are unfortunately all too common. One of the authors recalls being in a school assembly in

---

10   MacIntyre, 1971:24.

a British secondary school in which one of the senior staff read out John chapter 3 verse 16, "For God so loved the world that he gave his only begotten son". He proceeded to use this verse to make some point about obeying the school rules, leaning sternly over his lectern for emphasis. Evidently the appeal to the Bible was vaguely intended to add force to his message. However, what was memorable was not the actual point he made, but rather the sheer incongruity of the use to which the biblical text was put.

Misgivings about the use of Scripture to make educational points have been put in various ways. Some have argued that the Bible is about salvation rather than education, and that we should read it in accordance with its own central concerns. We should recognise that "the Bible is not primarily a pedagogical book. It therefore does not contain any well-developed theory of education".[11] If the Bible does not address a particular issue, then to try to make it do so is to distort it and deceive ourselves.

Others have argued that while the Bible does address all aspects of life, it does so from a particular angle, with a particular interest in our ultimate commitments.[12] So, for example, where the Old Testament describes the reigns of successive kings of Israel and Judah, it does so with a primary focus on whether they did good or evil in the eyes of the Lord, and not with the interests of the historian. Therefore some kings who had long and historically significant reigns are passed over quite briefly, their cultural achievements and foreign policy left unexplored. We should not, then, expect the Bible to directly address the details of a particular discipline, even though it might say something about its ultimate context.

In similar vein, Roy Clouser describes and criticises what he calls the "encyclopedic assumption". This is "the view that sacred Scripture contains inspired and thus infallible statements about virtually every conceivable subject matter".[13] It leads, Clouser argues, to a misguided search in the pages of Scripture for data relevant to every

---

11   Velten, 1995:68.

12   Olthuis, 1979, 1987.

13   Clouser, 1991:94. Clouser does in fact believe that Christian faith is relevant to all disciplines, but he sees this relevance in terms of fundamental presuppositions (see chapter 3) rather than detailed disciplinary information.

discipline. The search is misguided because the Bible was never intended to be an encyclopedia, and many of our questions are ones which it never intended to address.

This line of argument seems to suggest that the difficulties described above in applying the Bible to education arise because we are trying to make the Bible do something which it was never designed to do. This view is quite compatible with a high view of biblical authority – indeed it may be motivated by a high respect for the Bible and a desire to avoid distorting its message by bending it to our own ends.

It should also be noted, however, that these arguments leave us with some interesting questions. If we accept that the Bible does not simply tell us what to do in present day educational settings, or that it focuses on questions of ultimate commitment, or that it does not offer information on all subjects, does it nevertheless impinge upon educational reflection in some other, more adequate way? The authors cited in this section are concerned to guard against misuse of the Bible, but they would not see the Bible as having no connection at all with present day thought and practice. Are there better ways of understanding the relationship?

The Bible in the classroom

For those who begin to find the mounting objections daunting, there might seem to be some consolation in noting that the Bible remains itself an important object of study in educational settings. Studying the Bible is important for understanding not only the Christian faith, but also Western culture, which it has pervasively influenced. Many episodes of history, such as the Reformation, and many works of literature, such as Milton's *Paradise Lost*, cannot be understood without reference to the Bible. Controversies concerning human origins involve frequent appeal to the Bible. For these and many similar reasons, knowledge of the Bible remains an important ingredient in education, and the Bible may therefore still enter the classroom as an object of study.

This is indeed an important aspect of the Bible's relationship to education, but the consolation which it holds for those who hold the Bible to be God's word must be qualified. The Bible's influence upon culture has been a complex affair, and the myriad borrowings of biblical language, themes and imagery in Western culture have by no means always been particularly faithful to the biblical text itself.[14]

Moreover, even where this caution is noted and taken into account, the use of the Bible as educational content does not in and of itself imply that education is being *guided* by Scripture. Insects are also commonly part of the content covered in schools, and a particularly enthusiastic entomologist could no doubt develop materials liberally sprinkled with pictures of our six-legged friends. It would hardly follow that insects had authoritatively shaped the educational process. Including the Bible as content, or even liberally sprinkling worksheets with Bible verses, is no guarantee that the education offered is in any substantial sense 'biblical'.

Some have in fact argued that once the Bible passes from the hands of the believing community into the hands of the educator, then it passes into educational jurisdiction and must be subject to educational interests, rather than education being subject to the Bible. The claim is that the educational use of a biblical text is not the same as its use in the church context, and the interpretive concerns of the believing community should no longer hold sway.[15] The central concern is how the text used enhances the pupil's learning. If it fires his or her imagination and leads to a piece of writing which would be regarded as entirely heretical by the believing community, that may, it is argued, still be a highly successful educational outcome.

Anyone who is uncomfortable with the idea of the Bible being at the mercy of current educational ideas and fashions is returned to the question of what it might mean for the wider educational context to be faithful to Scripture – what would be a *biblical* use of the Bible in education? Considering the use of the Bible as content returns us to the very question with which we started.

Just a long-running delusion?

We have surveyed various difficulties which have been raised concerning the effort to connect education with the Bible. We have seen it alleged that we must choose between general principles from which

---

14   See Clines, 1997:31-54.
15   See e.g. Grimmitt, 1987, 1991 and, in response, Cooling, 1996.

little of substance follows and biblical specifics which are of dubious applicability to our present context. It has been suggested that the Bible may in any case not be designed to answer those educational questions which happen to be important to us in our particular context. Furthermore, the appearance of the Bible as an item of educational content is no guarantee that its role is an authoritative one. And yet Christian educators past and present have maintained that education must be illuminated by "the effulgent word of God",[16] that "biblical truth infuses every aspect of the Christian school's practice and curriculum".[17] Is this really no more than a long-running delusion? Or is there more to the relationship between the Bible and education than the arguments surveyed in this chapter would suggest? We believe that there is in fact a lot more to the relationship than even many of its Christian supporters suspect; the remaining chapters of this book are devoted to an exploration of the positive possibilities for linking the Bible fruitfully to the everyday design of teaching and learning.

---

16   J. A. Comenius, writing in the 17th century, cited from Keatinge, 1967:240.

17   Vryhof, Brouwer, Ulstein, & VanderArk, 1989:26.

3

The Word become flesh

I recall an occasion early in my teacher training when I was brought up short by the discrepancies between my work as a teacher and some particular sentences from the Bible. I had been enthused by reading some books calling for radically Christian thinking and gripped by their emphasis on being transformed by the renewing of my mind. I entered my teacher training course ready to subject the various theories which were taught to critical scrutiny. In my more arrogant moments I think I even saw myself as some kind of knight in shining armour riding out rather self-righteously in the cause of truth against the secular ideologies lurking in my education lectures.

Then one day I had to teach in a real classroom in a local secondary school. My teenage students were fractious and unimpressed by my unskilled eagerness. As if that were not enough, I also had a bruising encounter with the following text:

> Don't have anything to do with foolish and stupid arguments, because you know they produce quarrels. And the Lord's servant must not quarrel; instead he must be kind to everyone, able to teach, not resentful. Those who oppose him he must gently instruct ...[1]

Around the same time I came across a book which dwelt upon the warning in the epistle of James that "not many of you should presume to be teachers ... because you know that we who teach will be judged more strictly".[2] The author went on to offer a profile of the Christian teacher based on James' vision of true wisdom, which is "first of all pure; then peace-loving, considerate, submissive, full of mercy and good fruit, impartial and sincere".[3]

In those weeks my first frustrating, fumbling efforts at teaching teenagers tested my ability to remain civil, let alone gentle. Some were unruly, some were discourteous, some were openly keen to test the mettle of the new student teacher. One eleven-year-old boy stripped to the waist while I was writing on the blackboard, apparently just to see what I would do. Many evenings I returned home exasperated and discouraged. Given the yawning gap between my experience and what I was reading (kind to *everyone*? *Never* resentful? *Full* of mercy? Even with *that* class?), it did not take long for my reforming zeal to be humbled. Somehow *living* all of these qualities was a whole lot harder than solving intellectual puzzles; in addition to understanding, I needed grace.

I am sure that some of that gap still yawns, but I also trust that my ongoing efforts to drink from those texts have had some impact on the nature of my teaching. They immediately caused me to reflect on some of the teaching I saw around me. A colleague kept his classes in a state of awed submission which made me envious, but appeared to do so in large measure through the use of biting sarcasm when students stepped out of line. They came to fear the lash of his tongue. *Kind* to everyone? *Full of mercy*? These commanding words may not have told me exactly how to teach. They did, however, help me not only to realise that there were some character qualities that I needed to work on,

---

1   2 Timothy 2:23-25.

2   James 3:1; the book was May, 1988.

3   James 3:17.

but also to decide that there were some models of teaching which I did *not* wish to follow.

I doubt that these experiences are particularly unusual. They offer a place to start which focuses on everyday attempts by individual Christian teachers to live in the light of Scripture. Christians commonly read the Bible not so much with the aim of extracting useful theories as with the aim of drawing strength and inspiration and being shaped by what they read. They come seeking to make themselves vulnerable to the text, allowing it to speak to them with authority. They are willing for its promises and commands, its stories and images to shape their sense of self, their responses to events, and their interactions with others.

Here we have a first way of understanding the relationship between the Bible and present day education, a way which is likely to be second nature to most Christian teachers. People who read the Bible with a readiness for personal change will find that it has a great deal to say about the qualities which should be evident in their actions and relationships. Over time the Bible may shape their sense of self and of who they should be. If these people are also teachers, then this process is likely to have some impact on who they are when they are teaching. This will in turn affect the educational experience of their students. At this basic level, the bridge between the Bible and the present day classroom is not so much a set of deductions leading to general principles as the *teacher herself or himself*, shaped by interactions with the biblical text. Put simply, the Bible shapes people, and it is people who educate.

'Incarnating' the gospel

This approach to the relationship of the Bible to education is sometimes referred to as 'incarnational', drawing upon the central Christian affirmation that God has ultimately revealed himself not in a set of instructions or principles, but rather by becoming flesh in the person of Jesus Christ.[4] By analogy, and through Christ's indwelling, the Christian teacher should aspire to 'incarnate' the biblical vision, living it out in

---

4   See e.g. Badley, 1994, 1996. The benefits and dangers of such metaphorical uses of 'incarnational' terms will be discussed further in chapter 11.

the day to day interactions of the classroom. The daily process of Christian discipleship is in this way directly linked to growth as a teacher. This is therefore a natural way for many Christian teachers to think about the relationship between the Bible and education.

The strengths of this approach to the relationship between the Bible and education are not hard to identify. At the Bible's end of the relationship, such an emphasis seems to accord well with important biblical emphases. The New Testament is deeply interested in personal renewal, and speaks of believers becoming themselves a "letter from Christ ... written not with ink but with the Spirit of the living God, not on tablets of stone but on tablets of human hearts".[5] At the educational end the focus is placed immediately and squarely on concrete classroom realities, growing relationships between teachers and learners, and those daily acts of care which form such a significant part of educational processes. For students, the character of the teacher can play a huge role in the quality of the learning experience.

Some criticisms

Given these benefits, it may seem churlish to move immediately to some criticisms of 'incarnational' emphases. Criticisms there are, however, and they come from within the Christian community. These are, it should be noted, not criticisms of responsiveness to the Bible's call to love, but rather criticisms of a tendency to take an emphasis on personal character as sufficient and explore no further. There are at least three reasons for regarding a preoccupation with the effects of Bible reading on the individual character of the teacher as inadequate if taken alone.

The first reason has to do with *narrowness*. To reduce the impact of the Bible to the development of desirable character qualities in individuals is to truncate the Gospel, implying that it can transform individuals but has no significance for the wider world.[6] As many critics of overly individualistic forms of pietism have argued, to see the Bible as only addressing individual growth in biblical virtues, and having no contribution to make to our thinking about the content of the

---

5   2 Corinthians 3:3.

6   See e.g. Kuyper, 1931; Wolters, 1985.

curriculum or the teaching methodologies which currently predominate is to sell the Bible short. Does the Bible have nothing to say about the nature of the world we study or the nature of students or the values of the society for which they are being prepared? Do biblical warnings to seek justice or a renewed mind never entail rethinking what we teach and how we teach it? Teaching Christianly can all too easily be reduced to being a nice person, with little effort to think through broader educational issues. Faith and education may remain largely locked in parallel universes. If personal growth alone is emphasised it seems as if all that the Bible adds to secular education is the hope of having nicer people to deliver it.

This already implies a second danger, that of *complicity*. An overly narrow focus on personal graces would allow for the possibility of a Christian teacher displaying a loving attitude towards students, teaching with patience and humility, and in general exemplifying desirable character qualities while offering a curriculum full of untruths or ideological distortions. Imagine a teacher in Nazi Germany arguing that it is OK to educate learners to serve the *Führer* as long as she is nice to them in class and fair in her grading policies. Then consider how easy it is with hindsight to criticise such an extreme and stereotyped example, and ponder the question of whether our own cultures are free from tendencies against which Christians should protest. Would a pedagogy which refused to offer guidance to students in the name of their complete autonomy be acceptable for Christian teachers if administered in a gentle way, or should those teachers also be thinking Christianly about the nature of the learners they teach? Would a curriculum which taught or implied that human beings are at bottom nothing but a collection of chemicals be acceptable if the teacher were patient and kind? What if the personal virtues of the teacher in fact serve to make the teaching of falsehoods more effective? As Wright puts it, commenting on tendencies to focus narrowly on personal piety, "it would be perfectly possible to believe this 'gospel' and go off to work every day for years without noticing that one was building the tower of Babel."[7]

A third issue has to do with the *underdeveloped* nature of any 'incarnational' approach which tries to focus only on the teacher's individual character qualities. We will dwell on this point at greater length, since it leads us into considerations which will unfold in later

---

7   Wright, 1992:116.

chapters. A person-centred approach already raises wider questions; really taking it seriously already begins to push us towards wider issues and other ways of relating the Bible to education.

Taking things further

In the first place, we need to ask: is growth in the kinds of personal qualities mentioned earlier simply a kind of private interest, of concern only to the individual involved but irrelevant to the actual teaching and learning? Or is such growth important to the teacher *as a teacher*? If the former, then the Bible is not being related to education at all – its role in the teacher's life is on a par with her preferring fish for supper on Tuesdays. If the latter, if the Bible's influence on the teacher's character is relevant to the way he teaches, then the implications cannot be restricted to the individual teacher's personal morality. Believing that such character qualities as kindness, humility and gentleness are important to the being of the teacher *as teacher* already calls into question some ways of understanding teaching and learning.

There are, for instance, influential modern visions of education which view teaching as essentially a technical affair. The goals of learning should on these views be carefully defined in terms of empirically measurable behaviours; teachers must be trained in the correct techniques for reaching those goals, and provided that the teacher follows the techniques correctly and in the right order then the goals of learning will be achieved with the requisite efficiency.[8] This attempt to scientifically codify teacher and learner behaviours and to understand teaching as the rigorous application of a method, a "routine of efficiency",[9] does require of the teacher a certain discipline and diligence. It suggests, however, that more interpersonal virtues such as gentleness and kindness have little to do with learning. They may on occasion make the classroom a warmer place, but provided the teacher follows the right techniques the required results will follow in any case.

This vision of teaching as efficient technique can be contrasted with a view of education such as that of Parker Palmer, who argues

---

8   On this view of teaching see Davis, 1999; Dunne, 1993.
9   Ong, 1958:225.

that it is "the human heart that is the source of good teaching".[10] Palmer suggests that:

> good teachers possess a capacity for connectedness. They are able to weave a complex web of connections between themselves, their subjects and their students ... the connections made by good teachers are held not in their methods but in their hearts – meaning heart in its ancient sense, as the place where intellect and emotion and spirit and will converge in the human self.[11]

This approach seems to cohere better with a vital concern for the teacher's spiritual and moral growth, and its points of tension with the more technical view reveal how such a concern begins to compel us to move beyond a focus on the individual teacher towards a particular understanding of the teaching and learning process.

Once this process of reflection begins, it can lead to more detailed adjustments in pedagogy. I found myself involved in just such a process some years ago when I began to consider how a concern for honesty might affect the conversations I had with students in French lessons.[12] Since the rise of communicative approaches to foreign language teaching, it has become common to use personalised questions and activities for language practice – questions such as 'where do you live?' or tasks such as 'describe a recent vacation'. It is also common to encourage students, especially in exam situations, to invent details if they can't remember the foreign word for what they want to say. The point is to say some French, the argument goes, not to explain your family history. It's role play, not real communication.

The trouble is, a lot of communicative language teaching presents itself as a direct rehearsal for real communication. Students are often asked questions in the foreign language which are apparently direct requests for personal information: What is your name? What kind of music do you like? Where do you live? And so on. The New Testament urges that "each of you should put off falsehood and

---

10   Palmer, 1998:3.

11   Palmer, 1998:11.

12   This example is explored in more detail elsewhere, see Smith, 1997; Smith & Carvill, 2000:

speak truthfully to his neighbour".[13] One day I began to ask myself whether belief in the importance of honesty was consistent with encouraging my students to make up personal information when telling the truth was more difficult.

When I discussed the matter with colleagues, they raised objections to my scruples: should students not have a right to keep their own affairs private in the foreign language classroom? What if I asked what a student's father does and the father in question was absent or in prison? Was I not confusing what everyone knew was role play with the real thing? And would I not disadvantage weaker learners if I insisted on the truth, making it harder for them to say anything at all?

The complexities of classroom communication

It quickly became clear that the issue was more complex than I had at first imagined. However, I also noticed that it was not uncommon for students to ask, 'it's OK to lie in French, isn't it sir?' when they were working on activities which included the giving of personal information. Observing students carrying out language tasks encouraged me further to think that they often interpreted those tasks as genuine communication. I came to doubt whether they were as clear as their teachers imagined about the distinction between mere role play and genuine personal communication.

To cut a long story short, I began to make changes in the way I taught in order to make the distinction between truth and simulation more distinct while still protecting students' privacy. I began, for instance, to present certain writing activities in terms of a choice between personal communication or fiction. If I asked students to describe their family I would tell them that they could choose to describe their own family, in which case they should use all the resources available to find out how to do so accurately in French. Alternatively, they could write a fictional piece about an invented family, being as creative as possible. I also began to teach them linguistic strategies for politely deflecting unwelcome questions, an item

---

13   Ephesians 4:25. Baker ascribes to the early church "a basic ethic which views the demands of God to be embedded in believers' hearts and tested by every word they speak to their neighbours" (Baker, 1994:59).

which had not been on our syllabus.

The point here is that what began as reflection on personal integrity, in particular on the importance of honesty, ended in adjustments to my syllabus and teaching methods. A basic conviction that it is important to tell the truth even when it is inconvenient to do so turned out, when thought through over a year or so of teaching, to have implications for how I taught French. I became convinced that to value honesty for myself while teaching in a manner which undermined it was inconsistent.[14]

It was suggested above that an approach to relating the Bible to education which focuses only on the teacher's personal growth and the development of particular individual virtues is too narrow. It captures one essential side of Christian faith, namely a trust in God reflected in warm-hearted daily living, but it neglects the necessary complement of reflective beliefs. Examples like the ones just discussed suggest, however, that even this potentially narrow approach contains the seeds of wider issues, that if an 'incarnational' approach is really taken seriously it must lead to serious reflection on issues of curriculum and pedagogy. Commitment to a particular vision of human flourishing can lead to changes in how we teach. The next chapter will illustrate and develop this contention further, moving us towards a second way of understanding how the Bible can affect education.

---

14   For a similar example in relation to science teaching, see Cartwright, 1999.

From persons to propositions

Is virtue necessary to learning? Mark Schwehn argues that it is, and his argument will enable us to develop in more detail our contention in the last chapter that a desire to live out Christian virtues implicitly commits us to rethinking teaching and learning.

Schwehn argues that we should understand learning itself as in part a *moral* affair, and not simply a matter of technique or cognitive processes. Learning, he argues, "depends not simply upon the possession of certain cognitive skills but also upon the possession of moral dispositions or virtues that enable inquiry to proceed".[1] We should not therefore think of virtue as something added to learning in the form of character education, but rather as something intrinsic

---

1   Schwehn, 1993:44. Schwehn draws upon Palmer, 1983, and both authors are drawing from older Christian traditions which see learning in spiritual, rather than merely cognitive terms.

to learning. Any community of learning is informed by a certain ethos or spirit of inquiry. We should, Schwehn urges, examine this ethos and explore how the processes of learning depend upon the exercise of particular virtues.

He is particularly concerned to explore the social virtues, those which are bound up with "care taken with the lives and thoughts of others".[2] Humility is one example which he considers at length. He argues that an apparent lack of motivation among students may be rooted in a lack of humility. He cites an occasion when some of his students were reading a text from Augustine on friendship and loss. They concluded from a quick reading of the text that Augustine was just obscure and mistaken, and dismissed the passage as unworthy of further attention. Acknowledging that he may have failed as a teacher to motivate them, Schwehn nevertheless argues that:

> My students could have overcome my failings had they been sufficiently humble; had they presumed that Augustine's apparent obscurity was *their* problem, not his; and had they presumed that his apparent inconsistencies or excesses were not really the careless errors they took them to be. Humility on this account does not mean uncritical acceptance: it means, in practical terms, the *presumption* of wisdom and authority *in the author*.[3]

Without some measure of this kind of humility we are unlikely to learn much from a text which is initially difficult or which does not reinforce our existing ideas. Accordingly, Schwehn argues that "*Some* degree of humility is a precondition for learning".[4] Growth in humility could help with problems of motivation. It could also help prevent poor learning resulting from superficial interaction with the material under study.

Schwehn goes on to discuss the educational relevance of other virtues such as self-denial (being willing to relinquish cherished ideas in the light of new learning) and charity (reading the work of others carefully and in the light of their best intentions). He argues that we

---

2   Schwehn, 1993:44.
3   Schwehn, 1993:48.
4   Schwehn, 1993:49.

need a reorientation of learning which aims not simply at technical mastery, but at a reintegration of moral and intellectual virtues.

The controversiality of virtue

This might sound like an obviously worthy enterprise – who could object to an increase in charity and humility? Well, it is important to realise that the virtues which Schwehn discusses are not simply self-evident. As he points out, spirits of inquiry differ in their emphases and inspiration. He cites Enlightenment philosopher David Hume as an example of a thinker for whom some of the virtues discussed are deeply unattractive. Hume characterised qualities such as humility and self-denial as *vices* which "serve to no manner and purpose" since they do not advance our fortune in the world or contribute to our enjoyment. In a cultural context in which the Christian Scriptures have historically exerted a great deal of influence, advocacy of humility and charity can sound like stating the obvious. This is, however, far from being the case.

If we take a broad historical perspective we find further signs that Schwehn's virtues are controversial. Alasdair MacIntyre, for instance, catalogues the contrasts between the Bible's conception of virtue and the conception influentially expounded by Aristotle. He points out that "Aristotle, in considering the nature of friendship had concluded that a good man could not be the friend of a bad man ... But at the centre of biblical religion is the conception of a love for those who sin".[5] He adds that "there is no word in the Greek of Aristotle's age correctly translated 'sin', 'repentance' or 'charity'".[6] Perhaps most strikingly, humility, which is a central biblical virtue, seems to count as a vice for Aristotle, the opposing virtue being nobility of soul. The Christian and the classical strands in the fabric of Western culture do not speak with one voice.

Turning to present day educational debate we find that the virtues emphasised in the Bible remain controversial. Susan Mendus, for instance, argues in a recent article that while humility may be an attractive ideal, it is unavailable to us as a goal for education in a

---

5   MacIntyre, 1984:174.
6   MacIntyre, 1984:174.

modern liberal democracy. Our modern commitment is to qualities such as individual autonomy, self-affirmation, self-assertion and self-evaluation. She argues that the commitment of modern liberal culture to fostering such qualities through education is in tension with a genuine commitment to growth in humility.[7] As far as Mendus is concerned, it is humility which must, however regretfully, be sacrificed.

Virtues such as humility, charity and self-denial are deeply rooted in Scripture. "All of you, clothe yourselves with humility" urges the New Testament, "because 'God opposes the proud but gives grace to the humble'".[8] Schwehn in fact goes further not only to argue that the virtues he discusses are rooted in religious tradition, but to ask whether any resources other than religious ones can sustain them. Given that they have historically been sustained in communities of faith, are they likely to be sustainable under wholly secular auspices?[9] If the Bible fosters these virtues, and if these virtues are indeed controversial yet vital to learning, then the connection between the Bible and education envisaged here is far from incidental or superficial. We have here an instance of the Bible contributing something distinctive and substantial to educational reflection.

The shape of teaching

This contribution affects not only the teacher, but the shape of teaching. Schwehn refuses to reduce the virtues that he discusses to matters of individual morality. He recognises that taking them seriously will not only make demands on teachers in terms of their personal capacity for virtuous living. It also requires them to think through the formative effects which different ways of teaching and learning might have upon students. As he puts it, "to 'teach' these virtues means first to exemplify them, second to order life in the classroom and throughout the academic community in such a way that their exercise is seen and felt as an essential part of inquiry".[10]

---

7   Mendus, 1995. Mendus does not explore the possibility of forms of self-evaluation which could promote humility.

8   1 Peter 5:5, citing Proverbs 3:34.

9   Schwehn, 1993:57,63.

10   Schwehn, 1993:60.

If we take these virtues seriously, Schwehn says, we must first exemplify them. This resonates with the 'incarnational' emphasis described in chapter 3; talk of virtue tends to ring hollow if it is not accompanied by virtuous living. If we believe in a particular vision of what is good and right for human character and relationships, we must seek to live it out as educators in the classroom context. In doing so, we will be modelling it for students, wordlessly inviting them to aspire to and grow in the same character qualities. Teachers who wish to promote humility must themselves be open about the limits of their expertise, open to others' views and willing to confess failures.

But we should not stop there. We must also, Schwehn says, attend to the ways in which teaching and learning are ordered. We must examine the fruits of our ways of organising things, our ways of interacting with learners and with subject matter. We need, he argues, to order life in the classroom so that the desired virtues are supported and fostered. A classroom in which self-assertiveness is consistently rewarded with attention and success may do little to foster humility. If we rely on behaviouristic, drill-oriented teaching methods, we must ask ourselves whether they could possibly foster growth in charity. As in the French teaching example described in chapter three, we find our attention shifting from our own personal qualities as teachers to the approach to teaching and learning which is evident in our classroom.

If we believe that these virtues are important enough to be worked at in our own lives and modelled, then there would seem to be some inconsistency if we do not attend to how our teaching can foster or undermine them in our students. Questions of curriculum and pedagogy cannot then be excluded from the picture. This is not to say that the Bible has offered us a developed pedagogy or a set of answers to all of our questions about how to teach in present-day classrooms. It has, however, led to a certain set of questions, to an idea of the kind of inquiry that is needed and the kind of answers we are looking for. Schwehn's ideas thus confirm the point that we made in the last chapter, that an 'incarnational' emphasis on personal character spills over into a reshaping of teaching processes if it is taken seriously enough. However, we are also implicitly required to take another step further.

From a view of personal growth to a view of the world

One evening some years ago, while visiting a young biker who had recently come to faith and joined our church, one of the authors ended up in conversation with another visitor. He called himself Sprog, and was a young man who looked back with little affection on his school days. His school career had been prematurely curtailed when he was expelled for stealing. His own evaluation of his education and its inconsistencies was summed up in something like the following words: "They taught me that life was all about the survival of the fittest, then when I stole stuff they threw me out."

In Sprog's eyes at least, his school had failed to explore the connections between the vision of reality which it (perhaps only implicitly) promoted and the character qualities which it wanted to see in learners. Yet virtue does not stand in a vacuum. If the understanding of matters such as history, science, our use of natural or economic resources, or work and careers reflected in our curriculum is such that exercising humility or charity makes no ultimate sense, then virtue talk seems likely to ring hollow. If the content of the curriculum consistently implies that the purpose of money is to achieve a higher standard of living, that the heroes of history are those who succeeded in imposing their will, or that the weak are to be despised or ignored, the pursuit of certain virtues will lack plausibility.

There is debate concerning not only the list of virtues to be pursued, as we noted above, but also the meaning of virtuous behaviour. It has, for instance, been suggested that the existence of altruistic behaviour is connected to the limitations of human rationality in the face of a complex world. Some individuals tend to behave in a manner which does not contribute to their genetic fitness, i.e. their expected number of offspring. Herbert Simon has argued that this can be explained in terms of the evolutionary usefulness of people's tendency "to learn and believe what they perceive others in the society want them to learn and believe", and the human limitations on their ability to rationally examine every behaviour for its contribution to their genetic fitness.[11] Philosopher Alvin Plantinga has argued in response that Christians cannot accept such an explanation as adequate. If it is

---

11   Simon, 1990:1666.

true that living for God's glory fulfils our human nature and leads to eternal joy, then altruism must be seen as an example of supremely rational behaviour, not as a product of the limitations on our ability to weigh behaviours rationally.[12] It matters not only whether altruism-producing beliefs are socially useful, but also whether they are true.

Such debate leads us to the following question: would a curriculum which taught Simon's view of human behaviour as normative be likely to meet Schwehn's desire for teaching and learning to foster virtues such as humility and charity? Or would it be more likely to undermine such an attempt by leading learners to see such virtues as a result of the limits of human rationality? Having started from personal virtue, we find ourselves having to consider broader theories of human nature which may inform the school curriculum, theories which may affect the moral outcomes of education. The Good and the True turn out to be intimately connected.

Note that the focus now is on Christian *understanding* as much as Christian living. Plantinga's interest is in whether the content of Christian belief has discernible implications for the way we approach particular theories and ideas. As he explains in another essay, he sees the task of the Christian thinker as that of working out the implications of Christian beliefs for the subject matter of the various disciplines. This will involve working out and stating "a large number of propositions, each explicating the bearing of the faith on some part of the discipline in question".[13] In other words, we should be developing a body of propositions which state that if a certain Christian belief is the case, the consequences for our thinking about psychology or ethics or natural science or any other discipline will be such and such. Scientific theories should be scrutinised in the light of Christian belief.

Here we find a second approach to the Bible's relationship to education coming into view. We began from an approach in which it was the teacher himself or herself who provided the connecting link by 'incarnating' the biblical call to live in certain ways. Plantinga's views suggest a different link, made by working out the logical connections and dissonances between ideas about education and propositions derived from Christian belief. Our first approach

---

12   Plantinga, 1996.

13   Plantinga, 1990:60. Alternatively, Plantinga suggests, we could think of the result as "one enormously long proposition". See also Plantinga, 1998.

stressed the believing teacher's efforts to embody certain personal qualities inspired by a devotional reading of Scripture. This second approach stresses the need for the Christian educator to understand what the Bible teaches about the nature of the world and to work out what implications this has for education.

These two approaches are different, and are sometimes set over against one another. Advocates of consistent Christian *thinking* across the disciplines can show impatience with a privatised individual pietism. In turn they find themselves suspected of a dry and detached intellectualism which fails to foster personal devotion.[14] We have been concerned here to show that the two approaches are necessarily complementary. Taking virtue seriously leads us to questions requiring more systematic thinking; the more conceptual enterprise of rethinking the ideas underpinning the curriculum will in turn require 'incarnational' integrity. On Schwen's account, such rethinking will presuppose the exercise of certain virtues if it is to be done well. Moreover, the claim that altruistic behaviour is supremely rational will ring hollow if it hangs detached from daily living and contradicted by the teacher's own character. A view of how we should live and an understanding of the kind of world we live in are interdependent. Both can have educational consequences.

Relating Christian thinking to education

Having supplemented an 'incarnational' approach with a more propositional one we face new challenges. How does the connection between beliefs and their educational consequences actually work? We should, Plantinga argued, be developing a body of propositions of the form: if such and such a Christian belief is the case, then these things follow for our thinking about the world. What does it mean for an educational conclusion to 'follow' from Christian belief? After all, this was the central point attacked by Hirst. As we saw in chapter 2, he alleged that when we look closely, very few educational propositions can be said to follow strictly from Christian belief.

What Hirst seems to have had in mind was a relationship whereby a Christian belief logically *requires* a specific educational

---

14   See Badley, 1996.

conclusion. The educational conclusion is *deduced* as an unavoidable consequence from the Christian belief. This way of seeing the relationship seems to have two implications. First, it seems to imply that if there is such a thing as Christian thinking about an educational issue, then it will lead to one and only one correct conclusion, since that conclusion is required by the belief in question. Second, it implies that if we have stated the Christian belief correctly and done our deductions well, our educational conclusion will be as secure and authoritative as the Christian premise from which it unavoidably follows. If the belief is true and the logic sound, then the conclusion must be true and secure.

Now this is clearly a very strong way of stating the relationship between a Christian belief and an educational proposition. Unfortunately, if we state the relationship in these terms we quickly find that Hirst had a point; it is very difficult to show that a detailed educational proposal follows necessarily and unavoidably from Christian beliefs – as we saw in chapter 2, it is not even clear that support for schooling as an institution is strictly required by anything in the Bible. We need a more flexible account of how biblical beliefs might influence educational ideas and practices.

Approach, design, procedure

A helpful model of the role of beliefs in teaching can be found in a classic article published in 1963 by Edward Anthony.[15] Anthony argued that three levels of description are needed in order to make sense of a teaching sequence. At the lowest level are what Anthony referred to as 'techniques' and others have labelled 'procedures'. These are individual actions carried out by the teacher. They might include administering a quiz, showing an image, arranging the

---

15   Anthony, 1963. Anthony was not concerned with the role of Christian, or even religious belief, but rather with the long-running discussion among foreign language specialists concerning how to describe and define the differences between different teaching methodologies (see e.g. Brumfit, 1991; Kumaravadivelu, 1994; Larsen-Freeman, 1991; Prabhu, 1990). On this discussion and its relevance to Christian education see further Smith, 2000a, 2000b.

seating, or asking a question – in fact any single intentional act on the part of the teacher.

A casual visitor to a class sees mostly these individual actions. However, if he or she stays a while, it will become apparent that they do not occur randomly. Procedures are organised and patterned in certain ways, forming a way of teaching which has an overall consistency and direction. Individual procedures such as presenting words on a transparency, getting students to sort and reuse them, and reading a poem can come together to form a coherent sequence. This sequence or constellation of procedures was labelled 'method' by Anthony. A better term is 'design', which has the advantage of emphasising the teacher's creative agency in building a coherent sequence out of individual procedures.[16]

At the level of design some pattern and order emerges, but Anthony argued that we still do not have the whole picture. We still have to explain why the teacher chose this design and not another, this sequence of activities and not a different one. A design is in turn dependent on a wider framework of assumptions and beliefs; it is a way of realising a certain vision of things. The teacher's beliefs will influence the shape of the design. A teacher might, for instance, believe that it is of primary importance to make students feel emotionally secure in the classroom, and take relevant pedagogical steps to achieve this. Another teacher might believe that learning is mostly a matter of forming correct habits and teach accordingly. Anthony called this underlying network of beliefs an *approach*. In his words, an approach "states a point of view, a philosophy, an article of faith – something which one believes but cannot necessarily prove".[17] It might include a belief in basic human goodness or in the importance of humility. In sum, then, *procedures* are individual actions in the classroom, *designs* are repeatable patterns in the way teaching takes place, and *approaches* are the background beliefs, orientations and commitments which give rise to one pattern rather than another.

---

16   The change from 'method' to design' was proposed by Richards and Rodgers (Richards & Rodgers, 1982; Richards & Rodgers, 1986); see also Strain, 1986. Of course, if the teacher is closely following course materials, the creativity may be that of the course's author(s).

17   Anthony, 1963:64.

With this simple model in hand, we will delve further in the next chapter into the nature of an approach and the ways in which it shapes educational designs. As we do so, we will find the relationship between statements of Christian belief and educational proposals broadening out beyond the bounds of strict logical deduction. The role of belief in educational design is more complex than that, and also more productive.

5

Approaches to teaching

It is a weekday morning and a group of students in a local secondary school are in a foreign language lesson. Today they are practising the use of adjectives to describe people. The activity is taken from a manual of teaching techniques by Gertrude Moskowitz.[1] The teacher explains that often we feel shy of talking about all of our fine qualities, because others may think we are boasting. There are, however, occasions when we can legitimately praise ourselves. Each student is asked to imagine that he or she is going to give a speech before a group of people. The stranger who is to chair the event would like the speaker to draft a glowingly positive self-description which can be used for the introduction. Students are told that "they don't have to be modest but should point out all of the terrific things about themselves and be honest".[2] The

1   Moskowitz, 1978.
2   Moskowitz, 1978:82.

prepared introductions are brought to class, exchanged and read aloud.

Just down the road, students in a second classroom are also learning a foreign language, and are studying the very same parts of speech. They are working from a textbook called *Charis Deutsch*.[3] Their teacher presents on an overhead transparency various adjectives which could be used to describe character – honest, determined, foolish, serious etc. They practise these words in various ways and then are given a paper copy of the transparency. They are asked to draw a circle round words which they have heard others use to describe them, a rectangle round those which they would use to describe themselves, and a triangle round any which represent future aspirations. Once the vocabulary has been sorted, students are given the outline of a poem into which they can insert their words: "Other people say, 'You're … '", and so on. Finally, they read *Wer bin ich?*, a poem by Dietrich Bonhoeffer, a Lutheran pastor imprisoned in Germany during World War 2. In the poem Bonhoeffer describes the discrepancy between others' praise of his courage and calm and his own inner sense of distress and exhaustion. He finally leaves the question of who he really is in God's hands.

Beliefs in the classroom

These two classrooms illustrate Anthony's point, discussed in chapter 4, that different designs for learning are shaped by different approaches, with their different networks of belief. In both of these classrooms students are being offered particular models or scripts for their speaking in the new language. Each model is shaped by particular beliefs about human nature. Gertrude Moskowitz, the author of the first activity, emphasises that learners should focus only on their positive qualities, and that dwelling on the negative or adopting an attitude of self-denial are unacceptable.[4] The purpose of learning is for learners to explore their own selves and discover their inner goodness.[5] This particular activity (titled "Me Power") aims to achieve this by asking them to see themselves through the eyes of enthusiastic public praise.

---

3   Baker et al., 1998.

4   Moskowitz, 1978:2.

5   Cf. Moskowitz, 1982; Stevick, 1990.

The poem used in the second classroom is explicitly suspicious of such praise, and encourages learners to dwell on the discrepancies between what others say about them and their own experience of weakness and struggle. Its roots in Christian spirituality show through in its emphasis on self-examination, humility and our inability to understand ourselves clearly on our own. The activity is drawn from a Christian curriculum project designed to promote moral and spiritual development across the curriculum.[6]

The ways in which learning activities have been designed in the two classrooms show the influence of contrasting approaches informed by particular beliefs. It would, however, be too strong to say that the activities are logically required by those beliefs. Christian belief may imply that education should foster humility and self-examination, but it does not say exactly how this should be done, let alone prescribe the use of a poem by Bonhoeffer in a foreign language lesson. The same loose relationship holds between humanistic belief in human goodness and potential and the activities designed by Moskowitz. In each case a discernible approach has shaped the educational design, but not in a tightly deterministic manner. This chapter will explore some attempts to describe in more detail how this loose relationship between conviction and practice works. We will look first at some attempts to describe the role of beliefs in teaching, then at the creativity involved in applying beliefs, and finally at the tendency of beliefs to form connected patterns.

What's in an approach?

If we think of an approach as the whole collection of beliefs and assumptions which influence the teacher's designs for learning, then clearly an approach will include a variety of things. It will not only contain consciously held and articulated beliefs, but also a range of assumptions, often unconscious and simply taken for granted, drawn from past educational experience, cultural conditioning or the spirit of the age. In later chapters we will argue that it will also include images, narratives and models. For the present, however, we are interested in

---

6   The Charis Project. See www.stapleford-centre.org; Shortt, 2000; Smith, 1999.

the role of beliefs expressed propositionally as claims about reality.

Even if we narrow the focus to such beliefs, it would be mistaken to assume that they will all be of the same kind as Christian beliefs. A teacher may believe that trying to do discussion work last thing on a Friday is a waste of time, or that it is rude for students to speak without first raising a hand. Such beliefs, arising from experience or from institutional and cultural expectations, do not have the same scope and gravity as belief in the Trinity. What role might religious convictions play in this diverse mix of beliefs?

Nicholas Wolterstorff points out that while our thinking is influenced by various kinds of belief, that influence works at different levels. He distinguishes three roles which belief plays in our thinking in any given area.[7] First, we have a collection of beliefs about the world which we simply accept as relevant information. An example might be a teacher's belief that children prefer books with colour pictures to those without. We all have a large and varied collection of such beliefs about what is the case which we simply take as data to inform our thinking. Second, these are underpinned by what Wolterstorff terms "data-background beliefs".[8] These are beliefs which are a precondition of our accepting other beliefs as data. In the case of the teacher's belief about picture books, a connected data background belief might be the belief that the children observed by that teacher over the years are typical of children in general, or the belief that what the teacher has interpreted as signs of enjoyment were real and not feigned to win the teacher's approval. Such beliefs provide the context within which the belief that children prefer colour pictures is accepted as true.

The third role which Wolterstorff describes is the most important for our present discussion. When we try to think coherently about the

---

7   Wolterstorff, 1984, 1989, 1999. It is important to note that Wolterstorff is not claiming that particular beliefs always fulfil particular roles. A certain belief may on one occasion simply be taken as data, on another occasion it may function as a data-background belief, on a third occasion it may play a guiding role as a control belief, and on yet another occasion it may be that which we are submitting to critical scrutiny in the light of other beliefs (Wolterstorff, 1984:69). In other words, the fact that certain of our beliefs serve at various times as control beliefs does not mean that they cannot be subjected to critical examination on other occasions.

8   Wolterstorff, 1984:67.

world – or, more specifically, about what goes on in our classrooms – we face the task of trying to bring all of the information at our disposal into some kind of meaningful order. We typically find that there are a range of competing theories and viewpoints bidding for our allegiance, and we must weigh different possibilities. This is where some of our beliefs can come to play a guiding role, functioning, in Wolterstorff's terms, as "control beliefs". Control beliefs lead us to regard certain kinds of theory as acceptable or unacceptable. They may lead us to reject certain theories because they are in conflict with beliefs which play a guiding role in our thinking. Conversely, they may lead us to try to devise new theories which harmonise with them more successfully.

Take, for instance, beliefs about human nature, which have both varied widely and influenced education significantly. Are learners primarily intellectual beings or primarily emotional beings or neither? Are they complex biological machines who will respond predictably to the correct technology of teaching or spirited beings swayed by good and evil? Are they environmentally determined or individually responsible? Are they basically good, basically bad or some kind of mixture of the two? Is the ideal for the learner to achieve maximum autonomy, bowing to no outside authority, or is he or she fundamentally responsible to overarching truths and standards? Do we best find fulfilment in work, wealth, thinking or something else? Clearly, becoming committed to particular views here is likely to make certain approaches to teaching plausible or implausible. We have seen beliefs about human nature and human growth playing a guiding role in the examples described at the start of this chapter. Given that the nature of human persons is a matter about which the Bible and biblical theology have had much to say, this would seem to be one area where Christian belief will affect educational choices. Moreover, it is not the only area; other areas where Christian belief can play a guiding role include beliefs about morality, personal relationships, truth and meaning, the purpose of learning, the meaning of work, and so on.[9]

Talk of control beliefs can give rise to the mistaken impression that they tightly determine the thinking of those who hold them. This is not what Wolterstorff intends – they exert a guiding influence, but do not do all the work. Wolterstorff states that:

---

9   Marsden, 1997.

theories are not already there in the belief-content, just waiting to be extracted ... For the most part the Christian scholar has to obtain his theories by using the same capacities of imagination that scholars in general use ... the Bible cannot function as a black book of theories for the Christan scholar.[10]

Basic beliefs, including Christian beliefs drawn from the Bible, can and do influence our thinking about an activity such as education, but they will do so by providing direction rather than by showing us exactly what to do.

How beliefs constrain practice

If control beliefs do not provide us with a set of guaranteed deductions, how else do they constrain our designs? In an article responding to Hirst's criticisms of the idea of Christian education, R. T. Allen suggests that there are three other possible relationships between belief and practice which are more frequently applicable than a relationship of strict requirement.[11] Christianity, he points out, is not a detailed cultural code in the manner of Islam – it does not prescribe a detailed way of life, but rather allows believers of various cultures to differ in many details of their day to day living. We should therefore, Allen argues, not expect Christianity to entail a single set of detailed prescriptions for education, but should look for other relationships between belief and practice.

The first of these is *debarment*: a given Christian belief may disallow certain views or practices without necessarily specifying in detail what is to take their place. We saw an example of this in the last chapter in Plantinga's argument that Christian belief makes Simon's theory of altruistic behaviour (and, we might add, an approach to teaching based upon it) unacceptable. Allen offers the example of

---

10 Wolterstorff, 1984:77-78. The term 'control' seems to be intended somewhat in the sense it has in the context of a scientific experiment, when a 'control' experiment provides a check on the results of the investigation.

11 Allen, 1993; cf. Keller, 1989.

teaching the practice of astrology, which is included in some Indian curricula but would be excluded from a Christian curriculum.

The second relationship is *permission*: certain views of practices may be neither required nor debarred by Christian belief, but rather allowed. Teaching chess, arranging the desks in particular ways, asking students to work in pairs, or using videos would all, along with many other details of the school day, seem to fall under this heading.

The third relationship falls somewhere between requirement and permission. Allen calls it *commendation*: Christian belief requires that some of a set of practices be adopted, but does not specify exactly which ones should be chosen. Allen suggests that the Bible's affirmation of human bodily existence, as opposed to a gnostic rejection of the body, should lead us to expect schools to offer some form of physical education. The Bible does not, however, tell us whether to teach football, tennis or aerobics. A certain field of endeavour is commended to us, and within that field we are left to make wise choices in particular contexts. The New Testament injunction to think upon whatever is true, honest, just, pure, lovely or of good report seems to be a further example of commendation in something like Allen's sense.[12]

Allen thus widens the range of possible relationships between statements of Christian belief and educational practices beyond straightforward requirement. Like Wolterstorff, he allows for a looser pattern of relationships, but he also identifies some of the forms which these relationships can take. Christian belief does still play a role but it is one with fewer requirements and many permissions and commendations, a role comparable to that of a filter which lets clean fuel through into the engine while keeping out the dirt.[13]

Allen's filter image certainly loosens the deductive straitjacket which Hirst found so implausible. It is, however, in danger of suggesting that biblical beliefs are only relevant after the event. If Christian belief is a filter, not a pump, then it does not sound as if it actually contributes anything substantive; it simply allows good contributions from other sources to pass through unhindered and blocks that which is impure. Allen goes as far as to suggest that the filter will operate largely invisibly, and that a Christian curriculum and a "sensible secular curriculum" will "largely coincide". We do not gain any light on

---

12   Philippians 4:8.
13   Allen, 1993:19.

Wolterstorff's suggestion that our guiding beliefs may lead us to actively design theories or practices in certain ways.[14]

Building or digging?

Another approach to understanding the role of belief in relation to practice is to think in terms of examining existing practice and trying to uncover its *presuppositions*, its underlying assumptions.[15] This reverses the direction of inquiry. Instead of building up from premises to conclusions, it is more like the activity of an archeologist, digging from the surface remains of an old building down to its foundations in search of its original floorplan.[16] We might, for instance, look at a behaviouristic model of teaching with its emphasis on drill and habit formation. We might then identify and question its underlying assumption that learning is largely a matter of modifying outward behaviour by applying the right stimuli. Once such underlying assumptions are laid bare, their compatibility with Christian belief (for instance, the Christian belief that the 'heart', the person's spiritual centre, is the wellspring of behaviour) can be assessed.

Now note that this process is not straightforwardly reversible. Take a simple example. If you know that I have some German novels on my bookshelf, you also know that I have books on my bookshelf – the presence of some German novels presupposes (necessarily assumes) the presence of some books. But the reverse is not true – knowing that there are some books present is not enough to tell you whether any of them will be German or whether they will be novels. The inference only works in one direction.

The same appears to be true concerning the role of basic commitments and assumptions. Even where we cannot make deductions from a set of beliefs to a single necessary set of practices, we can work in the opposite direction. We can explore particular educational practices or theories and trace our way back to the underlying beliefs and assumptions which they seem to imply. We may eventually be able to see clearly how these beliefs and assumptions have played a shaping

---

14   See further Smith, 1995; Thiessen, 1997; Velten, 1995.
15   See e.g. Clouser, 1991.
16   Cf. Burrell, 1979.

role, and then begin to explore what changes might result if we started from different underlying beliefs. The Christian educator's task is on this account not simply one of starting with beliefs and working out their consequences, but rather a process of examining practices, uncovering assumptions, weighing them, and if necessary designing alternatives.

From logic to Shakespeare

This to and fro between belief and practice points us towards the significance of the middle layer in Anthony's model, the *design* of a stretch of teaching. In some cases we may be able to identify formal, logical relationships between statements of biblical belief and educational propositions. However, when beliefs inform a creative process of designing learning experiences, their role is often less formal and more supple and responsive to experience.

N. T. Wright has suggested an image which vividly captures this more creative role of belief.[17] He suggests that we understand the authority of the Bible in the light of the following analogy. Imagine, he suggests, that we had discovered a long-lost Shakespeare play, but that the manuscript was incomplete, containing only the first four acts. We want to stage the play, but feel that it would be inappropriate to write a fifth act once and for all, for that would be too presumptuous. Instead, we decide to give the play as it stands to a group of highly trained Shakespearean actors. Their task is to immerse themselves in the first four acts and then improvise a fifth act. This, Wright suggests, is a helpful picture for our attempts to live now in the light of the Bible.

On the one hand, the first four acts do not provide the actors with a detailed set of instructions for their final act. As Wright puts it, "the initial task of the actors ... will be to immerse themselves with full sympathy in the first four acts, but not merely so as to parrot what has already been said. They cannot go back and look up the right answers. Nor can they simply imitate the kinds of things that their particular character did in the early acts. A good fifth act will show a proper final

---

17   Wright, 1991; Wright, 1992; see also Walsh, 1996. The analogy, like all analogies, is of course imperfect. It includes, for instance, no parallel to the role of the Holy Spirit in relationship to Scripture.

development, not merely a repetition, of what went before."[18] The actors must take responsibility for their final act; the work is not all done for them in advance, and there is more than one possible outcome which could prove successful and satisfying.

On the other hand, the actors are not without guidance. The existing acts set constraints upon the improvisation and provide impulses in certain directions. Wright points out that "anyone could properly object to the new improvisation on the grounds that this or that character was now behaving inconsistently, or that this or that sub-plot or theme, adumbrated earlier, had not reached its proper resolution".[19] In other words, the more formal constraints discussed earlier still play their role, and creativity does not remove the need for consistency and careful thinking. In terms of our model of teaching, an approach constrains and guides but does not forestall the creative design work needed if good teaching is to result.

From atoms to patterns

A final point which should be noted is that starting from Anthony's three-layer model frees us from the idea that we must be searching for correlations between individual beliefs and individual practices in order to somehow end up with a set of Christian techniques. What we should be looking at instead is wider patterns of meaning.

This is true at both ends of the belief-practice relationship. When we engage in the kind of creative design work described by Wright we do not typically apply our beliefs one by one. Instead we come with a complex pattern of beliefs.[20] Many writers have come to talk about this broader web of beliefs as a worldview, a more or less coherent way of seeing and understanding the world.[21] Our worldview provides us

---

18 Wright, 1992:141.

19 Wright, 1991:18-19.

20 Cf. Quine & Ullian, 1970; Quine, 1963; Thiessen, 1990.

21 The term is not without its problems, and not everyone who is convinced of the influence of Christian belief in our theoretical thinking is ready to describe that influence in the language of worldviews (see e.g. Wolterstorff, 1989). Sometimes the term 'worldview' is used to refer to a circumscribed body of conscious beliefs, with the consequent idea

with an overall sense of what is plausible, of what we should reject and what we should take seriously. When we weigh educational alternatives we do not typically test whether a single practice is consistent with a single belief; rather we seek to make more complex judgements about whether certain practices 'fit' or 'comport' well with our a wider set of beliefs.[22]

Similarly, techniques are not best understood in individual isolation. Anthony argued that techniques, taken individually, have very little meaning; the casual visitor to a classroom who sees only a collection of individual techniques does not yet understand the meaning of what is happening. Meaning emerges when techniques are grouped and patterned in the light of particular convictions. The beliefs at work in the two classrooms described at the start of this chapter do not become evident in isolated acts such as asking students to prepare a speech or read a poem, for these acts could be given different contexts – the poem or the speech could, for instance, be held up for criticism or ridicule by the teacher. It is the overall patterning of individual techniques which adds belief-laden meaning.

Imagine a third classroom in which the teacher teaches the "Me Power" activity on Monday, follows it with the Bonhoeffer tasks on Tuesday, and on Wednesday asks the students to reflect critically on Monday's work in the light of what they read on Tuesday. An observer who only saw Monday's lesson might reasonably conclude that this

---

that a Christian worldview is a kind of basic summary of Christian doctrine concerning the nature of reality. Other writers see a worldview as something more instinctive, our underlying, unconscious ways of seeing and interacting with the world. In this case, a worldview is not simply a collection of beliefs or doctrines and it is less possible to state exactly what a Christian worldview would be in doctrinal terms. A worldview in this broader sense will include the metaphors, images, narratives and models which we explore in later chapters as well as a range of perceptions rooted in culture, history and upbringing, raising the question of whether, instead of a single Christian worldview, we should think in terms of the enculturation of Christian faith in a variety of culturally influenced worldviews. See further e.g. Griffioen, 1998; Klapwijk, 1989, 1991; Olthuis, 1985; Walsh, 2000; Wolters, 1989; Wolterstorff, 1989.

22   The latter is Wolterstorff's term. Wolterstorff, 1984:68.

teacher espoused humanistic beliefs concerning celebration of human potential and rejection of the category of sin. But observation of the pattern of teaching over the whole week would lead to a different picture. It is not the atomistic components of teaching which reflect the guiding role of beliefs, but the overall meaning-giving patterns which emerge over time.

Finally, if we consider the beliefs which we bring to teaching to be important, then we will not simply implement them blindly, without listening and learning from experience. To do so would be to exclude the possibility of learning that our teaching does not actually achieve what we think it does. Beliefs are not a blueprint to be stamped mechanically onto classroom reality. Suppose we design an activity such as the one involving the Bonhoeffer poem with the idea that we want students to engage in sober self-examination. If that goal is important to us, we will want to observe and listen to students to find out if that is in fact what happens. If it is not, we will have to go back to the drawing board and may have to reconsider our existing understanding of how our Christian beliefs impinge upon our teaching practices. Allowing faith to guide education does not mean that our beliefs have to be a rigid straitjacket; they can function as a living element in an ongoing process of responsive design, learning and redesign. This may be harder to pin down with clinical clarity than a narrower process of logical deduction, and it may seem more vulnerable than the idea of a blueprint fixed and guaranteed in advance, but it strikes much closer to the heart of teaching and learning.

6

Once upon a time …

In the 1890s, during the years surrounding the 400th anniversary of
Christopher Columbus's journey to the New World, a particular way of
telling Columbus's story came to prominence. According to this version, Columbus's fifteenth century peers, as well as the sailors on his
ships, believed the earth to be flat. This led them to the superstition
that if anyone sailed too far they might meet their doom by falling off
the end of the world. Against this background Columbus was cast as a
solitary hero, grasping with both hands his conviction that the Earth
was in fact round and so advancing the cause of scientific knowledge in
the face of the superstitions of his day. This story became "almost ortho-
dox among schoolchildren"; in fact it is largely invented.[1]

In reality the educated world of Columbus's day believed the earth
to be spherical, but disagreed about the size of the sphere. Columbus

---

1   Ihde, 1993:61.

was actually wrong on this point, and his false beliefs about the size of the earth led him to expect to reach Japan within three thousand miles of Spain. Why, then, should the story come to be told differently in the 1890s? Don Ihde points out that the context in the late nineteenth century was one of argument concerning the relationship between science and religion, and suggests that "the tale spread in the nineteenth century was part of what could be called progressivist mythology designed to show that religious people were superstitious; that science dispelled such superstition; and that such knowledge was progressive".[2] The Columbus story was retold in such a way as to make it an example of scientific enlightenment emerging out of religious superstition.

Of course this is but one of many tellings of the Columbus story, a story which has been told and heard in different ways as the beliefs of the tellers and hearers have shifted. Columbus has been at different times and for different hearers the representative of Christendom discovering the New World on behalf of Christian Europe, the representative of scientific progress overcoming superstition, and, more recently, the leading figure in the conquest and rape of America.[3] These various ways of telling the story are not merely different; they are in conflict. Both their plausibility in their own contexts and their conflict with other tellings of the story are grounded not merely in the bare 'facts', but also in the basic beliefs of their tellers and their hearers. Stories are not innocent.

The different ways in which stories can be told and heard makes story-telling a risky activity. Perhaps for that reason, some have argued that at least some kinds of story should be kept out of schooling as far as possible. The ancient philosopher Plato inaugurated a long tradition of distrusting literary stories on the grounds that they are

---

2   Ihde, 1993:62.

3   Cf. e.g. Todorov, 1983. Hauerwas claims that "no story grips the imagination of our educative practices more determinatively than 'Columbus discovered America' … Of course there can be disputes about whether Columbus was the first discoverer of the 'new world', or whether he really discovered what we now call 'America', but the main outline of that story is not questioned. It is the story that forms our education system, privileging as it does the necessary background we call Europe, the Holy Roman Empire, the Roman Empire, Greece, the role of science, the great philosophers, and so on." (Hauerwas, 1992:218).

several steps removed from the truth, they appeal to the passions rather than reason and they are frivolous rather than useful.[4] These ideas proved influential and enduring, and have been echoed by various Christian writers across the centuries.[5] Let's stick to the facts, some would say. Keep story-telling for the final lesson on Friday afternoon in primary schools and, in secondary schools, keep it within the bounds of language and literature lessons and well away from the factual and logical heart of education.[6]

In the next few chapters we will explore an alternative view which suggests that story can have a more important place in education than this. In fact it can play a pervasive role in giving meaning to learning, doing so in ways which bring our basic visions of life into play. Before returning to what gets taught in school, we will begin by considering how narrative is important to the whole of life, and why we should take it seriously.

Stories, stories everywhere

Stories are all around us in our daily lives and are of many kinds, many genres. From very early in life, we meet with fairy tales, fables, folk tales, myths, legends, epics, parables, allegories and many more besides. They have different settings, plot-lines and themes. We listen to them, read them, view them in plays and films, hear them in song, make them up, change them. They make us laugh, cry, reflect, imagine, lose ourselves.

Scholars disagree on which elements are essential to narrative as a literary form. Elements commonly listed include plot, echo, repetition, foreshadowing, contrast, irony, tension, conflict, and resolution. In the broadest sense, a narrative is an account provided by a narrator of characters and events moving in some pattern over time and space. In a narrower sense, the element of plot is added and the movement

---

4   Plato & Waterfield, 1994: section X.

5   See Ryken, 1979:13-18.

6   See chapter 9 on the importance of metaphor. Both narrative and metaphor have been regarded by some as decorative luxuries of which our language should be purged when we come to the factual heart of education.

over space and time is from conflict to resolution.[7]

Some of the stories that surround us can be short, even very short, but nevertheless quite significant. In his book *The End of Education*, Neil Postman refers to the basic stories which shape education as our 'gods' with a small 'g'. Writing of "some gods that fail", he argues that the majority of important television commercials "take the form of religious parables organized around a coherent theology". The stories which they contain offer a kind of religious education, introducing us to the lifestyle demanded by the gods of the age. He writes:

> Like all religious parables, these commercials put forward a concept of sin, intimations of the way to redemption, and a vision of Heaven. This will be obvious to those who have taken to heart the Parable of the Person with the Rotten Breath, the Parable of the Stupid Investor, the Parable of the Lost Traveler's Checks, the Parable of the Man Who Runs through Airports, or most of the hundreds of others that are part of our youth's religious education.[8]

We could add countless examples to Postman's list: the parable of the contented family with the gravy cubes, the parable of the man and woman who lived next door to each other and found happiness in instant coffee and, of course, the gospel good news that comes from the man who represents a fruit-canning company – "he say 'ye-e-es'!"! These stories surround most children from their earliest days, offering miniature narrative models of what it is to be successful or unsuccessful, desirable or undesirable, clever or stupid. Postman argues that they have a shaping role in our lives, teaching us to bow down to the god of consumership.

We are shaped and envisioned by story

The stories that surround us help to make us what we become. They shape our attitudes to life, form our ideals and supply our visions. They provide us with identity and ways of living. They furnish us

---

7   Cf. Fackre, 1984:5.

8   Postman, 1996:34.

with heroes and antiheroes. As Alasdair MacIntyre writes,

> It is through hearing stories about wicked stepmothers, lost children, good but misguided kings, wolves that suckle twin boys, youngest sons who receive no inheritance but must make their own way in the world and eldest sons [sic] who waste their inheritance on riotous living and go into exile to live with the swine, that children learn or mislearn both what a child and what a parent is, what the cast of characters may be in the drama into which they have been born and what the ways of the world are. Deprive children of stories and you leave them unscripted, anxious stutterers in their actions as in their words.[9]

MacIntyre describes those deprived of stories as "unscripted", lacking a sense of how life should go; it is perhaps more common for individuals to end up 'mis-scripted', presented mainly with unhealthy narrative models for life. One such was the actor Denzel Washington when he was a boy. He has said, in the course of an interview about his childhood as an African American brought up on the edge of the Bronx,

> How many heroes are there out there for us? When I was a kid there was nobody up there ... Who do you look up to? Doctors and astronauts? Or the pimps and dealers? ... The pimps had everything all of us wanted.[10]

Washington's mother scrimped and saved to put her son through a private education. He started to read and to realise "that there was a world out there with real heroes in it". He has gone on to make a career out of playing heroes, including Steve Biko in *Cry Freedom*, Malcolm X in the film of the same name, and, in *The Hurricane*, Ruben Carter, hero of a Bob Dylan song, who spent 20 years in prison for a crime he did not commit. The stutterer who lacked a healthy script found his heroes and he has learned to tell their stories as he interprets the scripts of such films as these.

---

9   MacIntyre, 1984:216.
10   Wynne Jones, 2000.

Stories are central to human understanding

Many recent writers have advanced the claim that, far from being merely pleasant diversions, stories are central to the way in which we structure our understanding of ourselves and others, of actions and events. They are part of the warp and woof of our language and thought, of our whole experience of the world and our way of living. We don't just enjoy them as escapes from normal activity, we think in stories, constantly telling and re-telling to ourselves the stories of our lives, our days, our careers, our communities. And we dream in stories, however chaotic these tales of the imagination may be at times. Whether waking or sleeping, characters and events are seen by us in patterns in space and time. We locate ourselves and one another and the things that happen to us and around us in narrative contexts.

Alasdair MacIntyre provides an example to show how narrative is basic to understanding human actions:

> I am standing waiting for a bus and the young man standing next to me suddenly says: 'The name of the common wild duck is *Histrionicus histrionicus histrionicus*.' There is no problem as to the meaning of the sentence he uttered: the problem is, how to answer the question, what was he doing in uttering it? We would render his action of utterance intelligible if one of the following turned out to be true. He has mistaken me for someone who yesterday had approached him in the library and asked: 'Do you by any chance know the Latin name of the common wild duck?' Or he has just come from a session with his psychotherapist who has urged him to break down his shyness by talking to strangers. 'But what shall I say?' 'Oh, anything at all.' Or he is a Soviet spy waiting at a pre-arranged rendezvous and uttering the ill-chosen code sentence which will identify him to his contact. In each case the act of utterance become(s) intelligible by finding its place in a narrative.[11]

The words spoken by the young man in MacIntyre's example are easy enough to understand: they have *meaning* but, without a narrative

---

context, they lack *meaningfulness* or point. We know what the young man is saying to us but we do not see the point of such an utterance until we can locate it within a narrative context.

N. T. Wright provides us with another striking example. He shows us that even factual statements about the natural world about us become meaningful when understood as part of a story:

> 'It's going to rain.' This is a fairly clear statement, but its meaning varies with the context. The context supplies an implicit narrative, and the force of the statement depends on the role that it plays within those different potential narratives. If we are about to have a picnic, the statement forms part of an implicit story which is about to become a minor tragedy instead of (as we had hoped) a minor comedy. If we are in East Africa, fearing another drought and consequent crop failure, the statement forms part of an implicit story in which imminent tragedy will give way to jubilation. If I told you three days ago that it would rain today, and you disbelieved me, the statement forms part of an implicit story in which my ability as a meteorologist is about to be vindicated, and your scepticism proves groundless. If we are Elijah and his servant on Mount Carmel, the sentence invokes a whole theological story: YHWH is the true god, and Elijah is his prophet. In each case, the single statement demands to be 'heard' within the context of a full implicit plot, a complete implicit narrative. The meaning of a word is the job it performs in a sentence; the meaning of a sentence is the job it performs within a *story*.[12]

The narrative, implicit or explicit, provides a framework for our understanding of individual statements, it allows us to give them a particular interpretation.[13] The absence of narrative leaves us not

---

12   Wright, 1996:198.

13   The importance of both narrative frameworks in general and of particular narrative frameworks can be seen in the field of biblical interpretation where, for example, canonical and gnostic gospels may overlap in making similar sounding statements that are seen very differently when

closer to the truth, but rather left with statements still awaiting the context within which they can be meaningfully interpreted. The same kind of phenomenon is present when we are presented with a set of pictures or a set of descriptive phrases: we immediately set about connecting them to form a story, a narrative that relates the pictures or phrases in some patterned way.[14]

Biography, history and big stories

Stories don't have to be fictional. Although we sometimes say 'That's just a story!' to indicate that we regard what we are being told as untrue or largely fanciful, we also talk quite meaningfully of 'true stories'. One of the most important true stories to any of us is the story of our own life. Ask someone who they are, and before long they will be telling stories. We locate ourselves in the stories of our lives. Other people are actors in our stories and, as we soon begin to realise, they have their own stories in which we are also actors.

Not only are there stories all about us, our stories and those of other people meeting, interacting, overlapping, and developing day by day, but we find that our individual story-ettes are parts of bigger and bigger stories, interwoven with the stories of our communities and traditions, of peoples and races. Stories point backwards and forwards and ever outwards beyond their present bounds.

In the sense of 'story' that we are using, the contents of a history book are story as, indeed, are those of items in news broadcasts. They are accounts resulting from the selective activity of a 'story-teller' which present events and characters moving in patterns in space and time. Stories are not only fictional; they can be efforts to tell it like it is. But as our earlier example of the life of Columbus shows, 'true' stories of biography or history can be told in different ways and heard in different ways.

---

placed within the framework of the story of God's actions in human history as compared with the gnostic emphasis on the hidden wisdom of particular sayings for which narrative context is merely incidental. Cf. Thiselton, 1992:152-3,165-6.

14   At the heart of the Thematic Apperception Test used in psychology is our propensity when presented with a picture to begin to construct a story around it.

This is particularly important when we find people purporting to tell us 'the story' of something. For example, if the story of human history is told as 'The Ascent of Man', a particular perspective is being adopted. The title says it all: the story is one of progress ever upwards through the efforts of human beings without recourse to the help of transcendent powers and, into the bargain, it is also likely to be the story of the male of the species.

Or somebody may purport to tell us 'The Story of Space Flight'. One way of doing this is to place it in the context of the story of ongoing human progress just mentioned. We might present students with pictures showing a more and more complex sequence of jet engines, culminating in today's space rockets. We might even supplement this with gripping narratives of young boys aspiring to escape the confines of their upbringing and reach for the stars, building their own homemade rockets and eventually getting to work for NASA.[15] Such a narrative affirms the impressive march of technological progress through human ingenuity. On the other hand, we might tell the story of how early rocket engines were developed by a team of scientists led by Wernher von Braun. The engines were designed to power the V-2 rocket, a long-range weapon used by Germany in World War 2, and in the latter stages of the war the labour used in their development was slave labour drawn from the concentration camps and working in horrific conditions.[16] At the end of the war von Braun, by then a major in the SS, and his scientific work were eagerly seized by America; he and other rocket scientists escaped the public scrutiny to which political and military leaders of the Nazi regime were subjected, and continued scientific careers with NASA. Here is a tale which does not consist only of noble aspirations and gleaming success; human invention, callous opportunism, and some of the most notorious instances of human

15   A recent bestselling example of such a story, in which Wernher von Braun figures as the author's childhood hero and the darker sides of his life story are alluded to only in passing, is *The Rocket Boys* (Hickam, 1998). The book has been made into a film (*October Sky*), student worksheets and quizzes related to the book are available on the internet, and a teachers' guide to assist with using the book in the school classroom is in preparation (information retrieved from the internet, http://www.homerhickam.com/teachers.htm, 18 June 2001).

16   See Neufeld, 1995.

evil went hand in hand. At stake in the different possible tellings of such a story is the question of whether technology is our hope for earthly progress or whether it too is subject to the drama of creation, fall and redemption.[17]

In Mathematics, the story of how probability and statistics were developed could similarly be told against different historical backgrounds. Given the historical connections between interest in probability and gambling, we could set the scene in terms of the mathematics of gambling. Perhaps a game of cards has had to be abruptly terminated; how would we work out how to divide up the money staked? On the other hand, we might choose to tell the story of John Graunt and the rise of an interest in calculating life expectancy for purposes such as life insurance. In that case we would focus on the early 'Bills of Mortality' which Graunt used to calculate the life expectancy of people at different ages in seventeenth century London.[18] Each of these different stories could plausibly make its way into a mathematics classroom, offered as the story of probability. One suggests a focus on the human condition and the ultimate facts of life and death; the other foregrounds the gods of chance.

The stories which frame the knowledge purveyed through schooling are not innocent; they are grounded in wider beliefs and priorities, and they offer to learners a certain way of seeing the world and their own future role within it. When we purport to tell *the* story of something, our Big Stories, those which encapsulate our background sense of life's meaning, are likely to be showing. These are the macro-stories, the meta-narratives, that underlie and pervade the smaller stories that we tell.

Examples of such meta-narratives are many. Postman lists a number in his book, from which we drew earlier in the chapter. They include "the great narrative known as 'inductive science'", the technology-god

---

17   Cf. Marx, 1995. On the different ways in which the story of technology can be told, and the tendency of technological celebration to be accompanied by a downplaying of the darker aspects of history, see also Segal, 1995; Staudenmaier, 1985.

18   In fact, these alternative starting points are related to rival definitions of probability itself, one a matter of the theoretical end-point of relative frequency as the total number of events increases and the other resting on the *a priori* notion of equally likely events.

that it has "spawned", the great story of democracy, and the narrative of "the great melting-pot" of the United States. Then there is the "god of Consumership", and the "god of Economic Utility" with which it is coupled.[19] We need such overarching narratives, Postman argues, for without them, life has no meaning, learning no purpose and, as Postman puts it, "schools are houses of detention, not attention".[20] But a great deal hangs on *which* narratives we choose to inhabit our curricula. Christian educators will find themselves asking how the biblical story of creation, fall and redemption relates to the narratives identified by Postman, and what its curricular implications might be. In our next chapter we will look more closely at the relationship between the curriculum and the competing stories that bid to shape it.

---

19   Postman, 1996:5, 7-9, 10-11, 13-14, 27-33, 50-58.

20   Postman, 1996:7.

7

Story and curriculum

Kieran Egan, in his book *Teaching as Storytelling*,[1] proposes that we see curriculum as a story told by teachers, a story composed of all the little stories associated with the various areas of learning and their many different topics. He puts this forward as an alternative to seeing curriculum in the traditional 'assembly line' way in terms of aims, objectives, content, method and evaluation. He argues that a story-telling approach is more true to how we learn and come to understand (something of which we saw in the previous chapter). Where Plato saw pitfalls, Egan sees potential – story can promote deeper learning because it engages the whole person, involving the imaginative and affective rather then solely the cognitive.[2] He argues that if curricular

---

1   Egan, 1988.
2   On this point see also Fernhout, 1997.

material is presented in story form instead of being couched as cold information, more children will learn better.

While Egan is not concerned with the biblical story, his work does raise in an interesting way the question of how our faith shapes our storytelling. Which stories should enter or inform our curriculum? Will any story do or do we face the necessity of hard choices? We begin this chapter with two pairs of stories that may be told in the school curriculum. They will face us immediately with the controversiality of curricular narratives.

Two pairs of stories

The first of these pairs comes from Egan. In teaching a unit on the topic of communities to six-year-old children, he suggests that a village/town/city may be portrayed in two very different ways. One tells a story of desperate and inventive survival, the other one of largely unseen and creeping destruction.

In the first, the children are led to think of the community as waking up one morning to find itself surrounded by a high, thick steel wall. The wall has the effect of totally cutting the community off from the world outside, including its water, electricity and telephone lines. The taken-for-granted comes to be seen in a new and different light. Food and water can no longer be assumed to be available. The community comes to be seen as "a machine which people have made to help our survival and fend off destruction", and the local supermarket "not as a routine prosaic aspect of community life, but as one of the wonders of the world ... a miracle of human ingenuity and organizational skill".[3]

He then moves on to suggest a different story which could be told to teach the same topic. This time the community is an organism, not a pleasant creature but a malevolent one which is out to consume and destroy in the interests of its own survival. At the beginning of the story, it is a small creature which settled down by the river but,

> As the years went by, it grew by drinking the pure water
> and dirtying it as it passed through and by eating away at

---

3   Postman, 1996:45,47.

the surrounding land. It became bigger and fatter and more monstrous, and grew faster and faster. It sent tentacles (roads) deep into the countryside to get food from more and more distant places to satisfy its ever-growing appetite, destroying the natural woods and meadows. Some tentacles ripped up the land to get minerals and fuels which it ate in its factories, dirtying further the land, air and water.[4]

A curriculum, even for six-year-old children and in a down-to-earth subject area, can tell different stories. Embedded in them lie different value positions, in this case celebration of the powers of human ingenuity versus lament for human destructiveness.

Another pair of examples comes from the teaching of biology with rather older students. The focus this time is not on stories that are actually told as such, but rather on the stories that may be implicit in our organisation and presentation of curriculum material. In a chapter in Mark Roques' book *Curriculum Unmasked*,[5] a teacher tells of an experience he had in his first teaching post in a large comprehensive school in England. He found that implicit messages were being imbibed by students through their experience of the whole curriculum. Where they met with conflicting implicit messages, they had to find a way of resolving the conflict in favour of one or the other. At the centre of his account is a series of booklets prepared by the teachers for use in biology lessons with twelve-year-old students. Their theme was the variety of living things and they looked first at fish and then moved on through amphibians, reptiles, birds and mammals. The teacher writes:

> The whole thrust of the study was evolutionary and as the pupils worked through the booklets the underlying message was "look how good fish are at turning into amphibia" and so forth ... the power of the hidden message was such that the pupils automatically assumed that the process was inevitable, unguided and within the time spans of their own experience ... life is a chance phenomenon, something that has developed through a

---

4   Postman, 1996:50-51.
5   Roques, 1989:161-164.

process of unguided evolution. None of my colleagues would ever have said this openly to their pupils, indeed a number of them were Christians and would have been horrified at the thought, but the way we put our curriculum together meant that our pupils imbibed (learnt is not the accurate way to describe the process since it bypassed their critical faculties) this particular message. And it implicitly undermined their confidence in God.[6]

Having discovered this undermining of confidence, not in a biology lesson but in a lesson in religious education which he also taught, the teacher raised the issue of implicit stories with his colleagues in the biology department. The ordering of the material in a particular way was leading the students to construct a story of a process which excluded God. The outcome of this discussion was that, as the teacher writes,

We simply looked for another biological principle that could be taught through a study of the variety of life, but which did not carry an implicitly anti-God message. We used the principle of adaptation so that the booklets now conveyed the notion "look how good the fish are at being fish" and so on. This perfectly acceptable biological message is compatible with, reinforces even, the Christian belief in the Creator God.[7]

Again, curriculum can tell more than one story, only this time we are concerned not with the overt use of the story form to deliver the curricular content, but rather with an implicit background story that influences how the material is arranged.

These pairs of examples give evidence of the range of stories that the curriculum may tell and that it may do so at all levels of education and in various individual subject-areas. In some respects these stories overlap, in others they conflict. Some are more compatible with the story the Bible tells us while others seem less so, even though they may at the same time convey truths and genuine insights. This brings us to the question of how the curriculum story can be biblical.

---

6   Roques, 1989:162-163.
7   Roques, 1989:164.

Telling the big story in the curriculum

What matters in all this is not primarily whether we use stories in our teaching, e.g. reading or telling Bible stories or other stories to our students. It is not so much what little story we tell in a unit of work or the syllabus for a subject-area. The deeper question is what larger account may be implicitly offered at the same time. What matters is which big stories, which meta-narratives, the students are being told explicitly or implicitly.[8]

We have already mentioned various alternative big stories – stories that speak of the glories of technological progress, the joys of consumption, the overriding importance of economic utility or the dangers of environmental degradation. Intersecting with these, now overlapping, now opposing, are the foundational stories of the human condition told by communities of faith. For orientation in this narrative melee Christians turn to the Big True Story of the Judaeo-Christian God and his actions in creation and redemption.

The Bible itself comes to us mainly in narrative form.[9] It is full of stories, and those parts of it that are not stories presuppose the true story that runs right through the book. Some of the stories are probably fiction, e.g. many if not all of the parables of Jesus. But they are told against a historical background, one of God's action in human history, and they are told to shed light on the larger true story told throughout Scripture. The Bible's story is both a mirror in which we see truth about ourselves and a window through which we see God and God's world out there, past, present and future. It is this biblical

---

8   It could be objected at this point that a narrative approach is simply a different name for an approach in terms of communicating a Christian worldview or of developing 'a Christian mind'. John Bolt has argued that it is more than these – see Bolt, 1993 especially his chapter 4 'The Christian Mind: Necessary but not Sufficient' and chapter 6 'The Christian Story and the Christian School'. In response, Harry Fernhout suggests that story is best understood as 'the matrix of a world view': a world view does not provide stories but, rather, "an embracing, plausibility-giving story provides a world view ... we could say that a world view is a kind of condensation or shorthand (a first ordering) of a life-shaping story" (Fernhout, 1997:85-86).

9   On the significance of this for theology, see Hauerwas & Jones, 1989.

big true story, the meta-narrative of creation, fall and redemption or, as one writer characterises the 'chapters' of the Christian story, 'God, Creation, Fall, Covenant, Jesus Christ, Church, Salvation, Consummation, God',[10] with which we are concerned in relating the Bible narratively to education.

The biblical story

Obviously Bible stories can form a direct part of the content of education. But what about all of the other stories which explicitly or implicitly make up the curriculum? How can a curriculum story be biblical? How does the biblical meta-narrative relate to all these alternative narratives or gods? Do they contain insights which are true and biblical (perhaps in part because they have arisen in cultures which have themselves been strongly influenced and shaped by the Bible) even if other elements and, in particular, their main thrust is neither true nor biblical? Again, on what basis do we choose among the stories on offer?

It is instructive to look at two writers whose work has figured prominently in our discussion, Egan and Postman. What do they have to say on the issue of which story to choose? In his *Teaching as Storytelling*, Egan looks for "educational criteria" for choice and these are mainly about meaningfulness (including affective meaningfulness), coherence, relevance and what he terms "the power of the story".[11] A good story, he suggests, should work with a binary set of opposing categories (such as success/failure or survival/destruction) which set up the initial conflict. It should then work with this tension and gradually move towards a resolution, taking care to exclude material which does not advance the story. Now all of this is helpful if what we are looking for is formal criteria for identifying an effectively told story. But what if our question concerns how to choose between competing stories which are both meaningful and relevant? How does the teacher decide whether to teach the human ingenuity version of Egan's lesson on community or the environmental destruction version? Here Egan does not really help us.

---

10   Gabriel Fackre points out that the story has a prologue and an epilogue and both of these are God – see Fackre, 1984:12-13.
11   Egan, 1988:24-25,29-31.

Postman clearly wishes us to reject some stories and adopt others. Those which we should reject are termed 'false gods'.[12] He promotes those which should take their place in terms of adequacy, meaning, purpose and identity. He writes,

> The purpose of a narrative is to give meaning to the world, not to describe it scientifically. The measure of a narrative's 'truth' or 'falsity' is in its consequences: Does it provide people with a sense of personal identity, a sense of community life, a basis for moral conduct, explanations of that which cannot be known?[13]

Although the criteria suggested by both Egan and Postman are of great importance, they do not fully address the question of which story is true, i.e. true to what is the case about human existence and purpose. This question is either being side-stepped or reduced to a matter of something other than truth. The fascist, communist and Nazi stories that Postman regards as "catastrophic narratives"[14] *did* provide people with a sense of meaning and identity and even gave them what they apparently took to be a basis for moral conduct. Perhaps this is why, when later in his book he puts forward "the fallen angel story"[15] (see further in the next section) and the importance of keeping "multiple narratives" in view, he brings in substantive moral values, appealing to the need to be humble and open to the possibility of being mistaken.[16] There seems to be a need for a more substantial place to stand if we are to discern which stories deserve retelling and which should be left on the shelf.

The fittingness of curriculum stories

As well as offering individual Bible stories which could become part of the content of curriculum, perhaps the Bible's larger story about human

---

12   See, for example, Postman, 1996:11.
13   Postman, 1996:7.
14   Postman, 1996:6.
15   Postman, 1996:66-70, 114-128.
16   Postman, 1996:67,60.

existence offers such a point of orientation. If (as we do in this book) we take the biblical meta-narrative to be true, we seem to have a standpoint from which it may be possible to judge the truth or falsity of competing narratives, although it does not follow that these competing narratives will be false in their entirety. How true or false they may be is a matter of how well they *fit* with the Big True Story of the Bible.

Consider again the image of Shakespearean actors working on the missing Act V of the play that we looked at earlier.[17] Some versions of Act V would not fit well with the master's Acts I to IV, while others would fit well with them. It is not a matter of proceeding deductively to a completely prescribed version, nor is it possible to reduce the sense of 'fit' to a single logical criterion. A whole range of possibilities are available and another whole range would be ruled out because of their mismatch. It is not simply a matter of the individual ingredients that could go into the final act, the characters, actions and events, but of the overall 'contours' of the story and a sense of rightness about its ending. Curriculum stories are true to the Big True Story in so far as they comport well with it.

There are ingredients in a number of the stories we have looked at which overlap with those of the biblical story. For example, Postman's 'fallen angel' story recognises the fallenness of human nature. On the other hand, he sees it mainly in a propensity to make mistakes, and he sees our angel-like quality in our capacity to correct our mistakes "provided that we proceed without hubris, pride or dogmatism; provided that we accept our cosmic status as the error-prone species".[18] As he describes it, this could be simply the outcome of our finiteness: we are limited in our knowledge and understanding and because of this we make mistakes. The biblical account of fallenness, on the other hand, is in terms of our sinfulness rather than our finiteness as creatures, of our rebellion against divine authority rather than our lack of omniscience. It is this that calls us not only to humility but also to repentance and faith.

Turning to the biology booklets, the 'Look how good fish are at being fish' story has ingredients in common with the 'Look how good fish are at turning into amphibians' one. It is even made up of the same information, the same facts about the capabilities of the various life

17   See chapter 5, pages 63-64.
18   Postman, 1996:67.

forms studied. However, the overall story is rather different. The first version has more in common with the story of the ascent of man, one of steady upward progress, than of God's creation of a world of wonderful variety and adaptation, a world now fallen but to be recreated by God at the end.

Contrasting narrative shapes

The idea of *shape* may be helpful here. The two stories told in the biology booklets may contain the same ingredients, but these have been patterned differently and so do not have the same contours. Change the shape of the story and the underlying message shifts.

A look at a well-known passage in Philippians chapter 2 could be instructive at this point. This is the hymn in verses 6 to 11 that tells of how Christ Jesus was in very nature God but did not think equality with God something to be grasped and made himself nothing. A number of commentators have suggested that this passage cannot be fully appreciated unless it is seen as a conscious play upon the Adam motif from Genesis chapters 1-3. Line by line, step by step, there is here a contrast with Adam as can be seen from the following chart:[19]

Adam	Christ
Made in the divine image	Being in the image of God
thought it	thought it not
a prize to be grasped at	a prize to be grasped at
to be as God;	To be as God;
and aspired to a reputation	and made himself of no reputation
and spurned being God's servant	and took upon Him the form of a servant
seeking to be in the likeness of God;	and was made in the likeness of men;
and being found in fashion as a man (of dust, now doomed),	and being found in fashion as a man (Rom. Viii. 3),
he exalted himself,	He humbled Himself,
and became disobedient unto death.	And became obedient unto death.
He was condemned and disgraced.	God highly exalted Him and gave Him the name and rank of Lord.

---

19   Thompson, 1998:18.

Now one could take these two columns and compare the statements made about Adam and about Christ one by one. But there is another kind of comparison to be made. The shape, the contours, of the story of the first Adam and that of the last Adam are completely different, indeed they are reverse images of one another. Where the first Adam seeks to raise himself to the heights of heaven, Christ steps down, down to the lowest place. Where the first Adam is brought low, Christ is raised to the heights. The one story starts low down, climbs in a proud curve and is then cast down lower than its beginning; the other begins in the heights, descends through humility and turns to soar up again into glory. The story of Christ forms a curve which is the exact inversion of that formed by Adam's story. Simply taking the statements made about Adam and Christ and comparing them one by one would miss this broader pattern. Behind the point-to-point comparison is an overall shape that comes through the details, and which must be grasped more by an intuitive judgment than a logical deduction.[20]

It is this element of *shape*, of patterning, that makes this approach to linking the Bible and education different from the more linear relationships that we have considered in approaches based on biblical statements or presuppositions. Different stories can carry conflicting shapes which express conflicting visions of life. The shape of one story can judge the shape of another, as in the case of Christ and Adam. We see another example when Jesus describes a rich man telling himself a self-congratulatory tale of growing wealth. Jesus opposes the steady upward incline of the rich man's tale with a story in which the rich man dies suddenly and mysteriously in the night – the upward slope is interrupted by a sudden cliff.[21] In fact a common feature of Jesus' teaching is the telling of stories which upset the tales that we are used to hearing and telling ourselves from day to day. If one story can judge another through its contrasting shape, then the distinctive contours of biblical narratives may call into question some of the stories about life which implicitly underpin the school curriculum. This is the process suggested by the examples discussed in the last two chapters.

---

20   Such more intuitive judgments are more to the fore in accounts of faith that emphasise the 'self-authenticating' nature of divine revelation. See Shortt, 1991; Wolterstorff, 1982.

21   Luke 12:16-20. Compare Jeremiah chapter 44 for a further example of narrative conflict.

Story can in its own right offer a point of connection between the Bible and the curriculum. But what are the characteristic promises and perils of proceeding by way of story? This will be the topic of our next chapter.

8

Promises and perils in story

Stories, stories everywhere. Stories surrounding us in our early childhood, shaping our sense of good and bad, of possibility and futility.
Stories beamed to our television screens, peddling their own visions of
life. Stories appearing in lessons across the school curriculum, and
deeper stories underpinning the design of the curriculum itself. It
seems that, as we seek to understand how visions of life shape learning, we cannot avoid reckoning with the power and influence of
stories. Should this excite us or worry us? Is it a cause for fear or celebration? Probably both.

Problems with unicorns

We discussed in the last chapter the issue facing Postman and Egan
concerning how we decide which stories to teach and which stories

are true. The profusion of competing stories offering different visions of life can seem to invite relativism, with no story any more widely reliable than any other. This would, however, be a somewhat premature conclusion; the Christian claim is that the Bible offers us not just additional stories, but true stories, in fact stories which help us judge the truth of other stories.[1] In any case the pursuit of more propositional statements of truth has hardly eliminated diversity and disagreement, so the problem is not unique to narrative. For Christians, the presence of competing spirits of the age invites discernment and a passionate and compassionate retelling of the biblical story.

There are, however, other worries which are relevant to our exploration of whether narrative can legitimately bridge between the Bible and education. Plato worried that narratives would inevitably lead us away from the truth. Christians are hardly in a position to agree, given Jesus' overwhelming preference for stories as the medium of his teaching. However, even if the story form is not in and of itself necessarily an enemy of truth, we should take seriously the fact that our familiarity with particular stories can not only enable learning, but also block it.

"When Marco Polo traveled to China," writes Umberto Eco, "he was obviously looking for unicorns."[2] Why? Because at that time and in his culture there were many tales current which took it for granted that unicorns existed and were to be found in far-off, exotic countries. When he visited Java and saw an animal with a single horn on its muzzle, he naturally identified it as a unicorn. He had to report, however, that unicorns did not in fact look as they were described in the stories: they were black, rather than white, had a head resembling a boar and feet like those of an elephant. He was in fact describing a rhinoceros, but he had been so conditioned by the stories he knew that instead of acknowledging it as a new, unknown kind of animal, he laboured to make it fit with his existing knowledge of unicorns. Eco comments that Marco Polo "could only refer to what he already knew and expected to meet. He was victim of his background books."[3]

Our stories can lead us astray, drawing us to work at forcing the world into the contours of our favourite tales instead of fitting our tales to the truth. Christians are hardly immune to this tendency. It

---

1   Cf. Wolterstorff, 1995:103.
2   Eco, 1999:71.
3   Eco, 1999:72.

was long believed, for example, that the story of the sun standing still during Joshua's battle against the Amorites (Joshua 10) taught us that the sun must orbit the earth. We are now aware that this is not the case, and so we read that story differently; but can we be sure that none of our other familiar stories are working together with our ignorance to lead us astray?

The seductions of narrative

Of course it might be replied here that we simply need to be more careful about distinguishing true stories from false ones. Things may not, however, be quite so simple. Postman suggests that all the narratives he lists in his book are 'imperfect' and 'even dangerous'.[4] His concern reflects an awareness, typical also of many postmodern thinkers, that we are not simply innocent victims of imperfect stories. We often *like* to have reality falsified in ways that please us, and are capable of twisting even true stories to our own benefit – as Paul puts it, we "suppress the truth in unrighteousness".

This suggests that the problem is not just that we don't know enough. When a false picture offered by an appealing tale legitimises our domination of others and makes us feel good about ourselves into the bargain, we are only too gladly led astray. As Amos Wilder puts it:

> many popular as well as more pretentious novels are fraudulent … because writer and reader conspire to dream a world in accordance with their own wishes or resentments … There are various kinds of traps which the true storyteller must overcome. Language has its inertia; narrative has seductions; the heart has its idols.[5]

Stories – even the biblical story – can be used in a self-serving manner. The Christian story can be told in such a way as to confirm our own prejudices and mask our sins – our love of wealth, our taste for being right, our low opinion of some other individual or group. The intertwining of the Christian story with the story of Western progress

---

4   Postman, 1996:11.
5   Wilder, 1983:364.

has led to missions based on the prior assumption that the receiving culture is entirely inferior. Bruce Olson reports of his first meeting with the natives of the upper reaches of the Orinoco River that they felt that the converts to Christianity among their tribe did not care about them any more. When he asked why, he was told:

> Why, they've rejected everything about us ... They won't sing our songs now. They sing those weird, wailing songs that are all out of tune and don't make sense. And the construction which they call a church! Have you seen their church? It's square! How can God be in a square church? Round is perfect ... It has no ending, like God. But the Christians, their God has points all over, bristling at us. And how those Christians dress! Such foolish clothes ...[6]

The Christian converts had been taught how to dress in clothes with buttons, how to wear shoes, how to sing Western songs, on the assumption that all of this somehow went with coming to faith.

But cultural insensitivity is not the only result of big stories being wielded in an oppressive manner. This is pithily illustrated by a South African saying: "When the white man came to our country he had the Bible and we had the land. The white man said to us, 'Let us pray'. After the prayer, the white man had the land and we had the Bible."[7] The bringing of the biblical big story to the African seems to be linked with oppression. A particular reading of the story of the tower of Babel in Genesis chapter 11 played a role in the ideological justification of apartheid policies in South Africa.[8] And think back to the various versions of the Columbus story described at the start of chapter 6 – Christian teachers would hardly be well advised to revert to the telling of this story as simply a tale of the brave Christian adventurer extending the kingdom of Christ. Believing in the seriousness of sin, Christians of all people should be aware of the very real potential for our storytelling (including our retelling of biblical stories) to be bent to

---

6   Olson, 1973:50-51.

7   This saying is recorded in Goldingay, 1994:91, but the writer refers it back to Mofeking, 1988.

8   See Cloete & Smit, 1994.

our own ends in the name of God's big story. In the same manner we need to be aware of the potential for our curricular stories to paint the world as we would like to think it is and evade the hard questions which reality might put to us.

Should this deter us from bringing biblical narrative into contact with our designs for teaching and learning? Surely not; if the problem is with our own impulses towards self-serving thinking, then it may infect any of the narratives which structure our curriculum, and excluding the Bible will hardly remove the issue. In fact, the Bible may help us at precisely this point.

Biblical criticism of religious stories

Unlike those competing narratives which encourage us to believe in human potential and rest secure in human knowledge, the Bible tells a story of sinful beings who have chosen pride over love and have an ingrained habit of suppressing the truth, to the point where we will murder our Saviour. It invites us to consider how sin may affect our thinking as well as our doing.[9] What's more, it contains within itself examples of stories, even biblical stories about God, being distorted to serve our own interests. In Jeremiah chapter 7, for instance, we find the prophet Jeremiah standing against the religious leaders in Jerusalem. The leaders are busy retelling a story drawn (if selectively) from many Old Testament texts (see e.g. Psalm 132). Their narrative focuses on God's residence in the temple. God chose Zion as his dwelling place, this story goes, and promised to live in the temple here forever, in the midst of the people he has chosen. We, the chosen people, are therefore safe from disaster as long as we continue to worship at the temple and bring the daily sacrifices that God required. Jeremiah's story is radically different: yes, God chose us and promised to dwell with us, but only if we obey all of his commands. Given the treatment meted out to the weak and vulnerable in the community, the

---

9   See, for example, Plantinga, 1982; Wolterstorff, 1981. See also chapter 4 of Shortt, 1991. This should lead to a proper humility and openness to others as, for example, Paulo Freire advocates in his talk of dialogical relations between teacher-students and student-teachers in chapter 2 of Freire, 1996b.

dishonesty, greed and unfaithfulness, God is prepared to utterly disown the sacrifices offered at the temple.[10] In fact unless there is a radical change he will destroy the temple itself and hand his people over to the heathen. The benefit of hindsight should not blind us to the fact that the story told by the leaders was the religious orthodoxy of the day, while that offered by Jeremiah was sacrilegious, unthinkable.[11]

We see the same telling of shocking stories in the ministry of Jesus. Here again our familiarity and hindsight can obscure the sheer outrageousness of stories such as the one in which a corrupt tax collector who barely knows how to pray goes home from the temple justified before God, while one of the religious leaders, a Pharisee, remains unaccepted even after all the appropriate prayers and observances. While the stories of the Bible, and even its bigger overarching story, can become captive to our own complacency, they can also speak tellingly to that complacency. Story can confront us with what we are like, acting as a mirror to show us our warts and all the hidden depths of our being. Shakespeare's Hamlet said, 'The play's the thing wherein I'll catch the conscience of the king'.[12] Centuries earlier, as recorded in 2 Samuel chapter 12 verses 1 to 14, Nathan the prophet told King David a story about a rich man who took from the poor man everything he had, one little ewe lamb that was like a daughter to him: Nathan's story engaged the king's attention and also caught his conscience.

It is also worth noting that the Bible models for us not only a critical questioning of fossilised versions of its own story, but also multiple retellings of the same story. From the parallel narratives of the post-Exodus wanderings or the Israelite monarchy to the provision of not one, but four Gospel accounts of Jesus' life, each with its own particular theological emphases, the internal diversity of Scripture may also be suggestive for our educational use of story.

The Bible gives us ample warning of our sinful tendency to distort the truth, and surely invites us to have these warnings clearly in mind if we try to allow the biblical story to frame and inform our educational projects. Any such effort must be accompanied by a considerable

---

10   See Jeremiah 7:22. (The word 'just' in the NIV is an interpretive addition to the text.)

11   For a further example see Jeremiah 44.

12   Shakespeare, Hamlet, Act II, Scene 2.

amount of self-examination if it is not to lead to a curriculum which 'dream[s] a world in accordance with [our] own wishes or resentments'. We need to allow the Bible to continue to stand over against our interpretations of it. As Brian Walsh puts it,

> Biblical reflection is foundational to all of Christian life, education included. But this requires an ongoing serious, passionate and loving engagement with Scripture. And this must be an engagement that allows our reading of Scripture to be full of questions and to be patient enough not to demand answers too quickly … What I am talking about is an indwelling of the biblical narrative in such a way that this story, with all of its tensions, plot confusions and dead-ends, and in all of its historical oddities, is, nonetheless our story. We find our identity as the people of God in this narrative, it shapes our character and it forms our vision.[13]

And in this process of indwelling, we interpret the book and, Walsh goes on to say, 'interpretation is something people do in community, in relation to tradition and in a particular time and place'[14] rather than with a once-and-for-all-time finality.

Having soberly considered the challenges facing their own storytelling, Christians should, however, insist that this warning also be heard by secular educators. The biblical story does not only suggest the need for some ongoing discomfort among believers. It also poses a pointed challenge to non-believers whose curricula dream a world immune to the presence of God and imagine a daily practice of life that has no need to take that presence into account. The Bible insists that this is a major instance of a self-serving, oppressively distorted narrative. In the Christian school context, where a version of the Christian story has pride of place, it is Christian teachers whose consciences need to remain soft. In secular contexts, where other worldviews provide the dominant frame and work to exclude their rivals, there is a need to hear the biblical story's eloquent depictions of the dangers of unbelief.

---

13   Walsh, 2000:112.
14   Walsh, 2000:112.

Some other perils and promises

Implicit in much of the above is a great strength of narrative, one which corresponds directly to its dangers. One reason why stories can be so seductive is because they appeal to us so effectively. Story appeals to us holistically: it engages us as whole people rather than making simple appeal to our cognitive faculties. It offers us models to follow, characters who embody possibilities, positive or negative, who inspire us to better things or warn us against worse. It offers us a world in which to explore courses of action best not tried out in practice. It communicates through what it does not say as well as what it does say, through assumptions and suggestions, sometimes by leaving something vital unsaid.[15] It can be far more accessible to a wider variety of learners than an analysis and comparison of abstracted principles and truths.[16] In short, the seductions of narrative come from its power to sway and inspire us, and are therefore potentially a force for good as well as for evil.[17]

---

15   Compare Moberly's comments on 2 Kings 2: "The sense of divine purpose and guidance is almost overwhelming, yet God himself remains constantly as it were offstage (the only partial exception being in verse 11). God is strongly present, and yet remains hidden. It is through a masterful use of the possibilities of narrative presentation that the writer has conveyed these effects." (Moberly, 1986:78).

16   This is argued as a major benefit by Egan (1988). Jerome Bruner says that narrative "triggers presuppositions" and thereby means more than it says, whereas the more traditional way of knowing "eschews or blocks the triggering of presuppositions and renders them as transparent as possible ... substitutes entailments in place of presuppositions" (Bruner, 1985:108-109).

17   Fernhout, following Wolterstorff, argues that a defect of some ways of using the notions of a 'Christian worldview' and a 'Christian mind' to frame Christian education is that these constructs place the emphasis too much on the cognitive, on the intellectual, on understanding the right things. As a result they tend to inadequately address community, the emotions, the role of celebration and lament, the actual brokenness of the world as it emerges in our experience (as opposed to our doctrines), and the diversity of gifts present in the classroom. Fernhout argues that a recasting of our idea of a 'Christian worldview' in the light of narrative goes some way towards addressing these concerns (Fernhout, 1997).

Story can also shift the emphasis from rules and precepts to virtues, as it focuses on the kind of persons we are called to become (or not to become). Rather than the rational weighing of abstract principles at the centre of the moral life, story allows us to engage with real people in their stories and particularly with the human being Who alone lived a perfect life. His story calls us to *follow*, to be and to become rather than just to do and decide.

A focus on story is also less individualistic and more community-centred and tradition-centred than our more didactic approaches to teaching and learning often tend to be. D. John Lee, writing of his experience of growing up as a Chinese Canadian, says, "The flip side of the question 'Who am I?' is another question: 'Who are my people?' Or, narratively speaking, my character cannot be understood apart from other characters in my story."[18] A narratival approach to curriculum can therefore help the student see that he is not an island, alone on a wide wide sea, but part of a mainland with a history, of a people with all their overlapping stories. We need not be, as the folksong puts it, orphans in a day of no tomorrows, but rather children of promise.

This note of promise points us towards another important benefit which a focus on the biblical story can bring to our educational deliberations. Harry Fernhout talks of the 'beckoning' aspect of the big story and he continues:

> The element of *vision* or critical imagination is deeply rooted in memory … But … the focus is not on what has been but what ought to be … A world view story, by providing its adherents with the resources to envision something different and better, inspires people to live towards that vision. This dynamic is clearly visible, for example, in the writings of the Old Testament prophets.
>
> Because it is oriented to what ought to be, vision has the quality of being critical of both the present and the past. In a story-formed world view, then, the present moment of a community or culture stands in a creative tension between the resources of memory and the critique of vision.[19]

---

18 Lee, 1993:14-15.
19 Fernhout, 1997:86-87.

In other words, a story is more than a collection of timeless pieces of information because it moves from past to future, from memory to vision.[20] It can therefore offer us not just individual items to consider, but a sense of direction, an orientation within time and history, an image of where we have come from and where we might be headed. It places before us the question of what is worth remembering and for what we should hope.

Some recent writers have drawn attention to the variety of 'speech-acts' that the Bible gives expression to, by no means all of which are acts of making descriptive statements.[21] Anthony Thiselton suggests that the 'paradigmatic speech-act' of the Bible is that of promise.[22] The story has an ending in a new heavens and a new earth and this is not simply *foretold* by God but *promised* by him.[23] The biblical big story of history moving towards such a promised end is, however, to be distinguished sharply from what is often termed 'the myth of progress'. As Richard Bauckham and Trevor Hart put it:

---

20   See also Groome, 1980, 1991.

21   See, for example, Wolterstorff, 1995, especially pages 19-94. See also Anthony Thiselton, who writes: "The biblical writings cannot be reduced to a Cartesian textbook of information that permits the response of only wooden replication of ideas or idiosyncratic novelty outside the clear boundaries of the text. Moreover, the biblical writings perform acts of declaration, proclamation, promise, verdict, pardon, liberation, commission, appointment, praise, confession, acclamation, and celebration that burst beyond the uniform model of flat 'information'." (Thiselton, 1999:153). He also points out that a whole range of speech-acts may be expressed in a single short passage, e.g. Hebrews 1:1-4, the words of which, as he puts it, "… perform several multilayered, multidirectional actions: … sermon, creed, confession, hymn, praise, acclamation, exposition, argument, celebration" (Thiselton, 1999:146).

22   Thiselton, 1999:223-239.

23   This is not always signalled by the use of the word 'promise': the use of another verb in the future tense "in an appropriate context of utterance (of situation, speaker, and addressee) may in fact constitute a promissory act" (Thiselton, 1999:223).

Unlike the myth of progress, Christian eschatology does not privilege future history over past history. The end of history will happen to all of history. In the resurrection all the dead of all history will rise to judgement and life in the new creation ... The countless victims of history, those whose lives were torture and scarcely lived at all, are not to be forgotten but remembered in hope of the resurrection. From this metanarrative the past is not another country from which we have travelled so far that it is of no more relevance to us. Knowing that all generations have a future in God's new creation, we practise solidarity with their sufferings, their achievements and their hopes, telling their stories as still relevant parts of the grand narrative of God's love for the world, past in which we may still find future.[24]

The distinctive biblical emphasis on hope, as opposed to humanistic optimism or pessimism, has significance for the curriculum, for the whole and not only for particular subject areas like science and history. On these terms history is seen not as the story of man ever seeking on his own to ascend to higher levels of achievement, according to which we now 'know better' than did those in other ages, but as a story of God's reaching out to rebellious humankind. Scientific progress is not itself the source of hope. The world of nature has a future so that care for the environment is not a vain effort to hold back the tide of destruction. Human beings, from whatever period of history, share in the same human condition and have the same significance in the eyes of God. Pain and suffering are real but passing so we neither turn from them indifferently nor provide care hopelessly.

Being aware of the dangers and making much of the benefits, the Christian educator can find in narrative a very important strand to the rope that links her faith with her activity as a teacher. At the one end it does justice to the Bible as a text made up in significant measure of narrative. At the other end it connects richly with our experience of selfhood, of understanding, and of needing a sense of orientation to the past and the future. The different overall patterns offered by different stories mean that the biblical story has something distinctive to

---

24   Bauckham, 1999:39-40. See also Wells, 1998:149.

contribute to the organisation of learning. The examples in this and the previous two chapters show this clearly, whether they concern ways of telling the story of Columbus, the history of humanity, the story of space flight, the early development of probability theory in mathematics, the portrayal of the village/town/city community, or the shape of the stories told in a series of biology booklets.

At the same time story complements, rather than replaces, the approaches discussed in earlier chapters. As Metz writes, "There is a time for storytelling and there is a time for argument".[25] And *telling* the story is not a matter of words only, but also of how well the words comport with the life of the teller; the curriculum story is not fully 'biblical' if it is not incarnated in the life of the teller. Story adds another strand to our rope; there are yet more to come.

---

25   Johann Batist Metz, quoted in Fackre, 1983:340. Jerome Bruner writes of two main modes of thought: what he terms the 'paradigmatic' mode and the narrative mode – see Bruner, 1985; also Bruner, 1996. Others have talked of 'recognition' and 'cognition'; see Fackre, 1983:342.

9

Teaching as gardening

For John Amos Comenius, teaching was a form of gardening. The great seventeenth century Moravian educator regularly writes of learners as plants, learning as organic growth and the educational setting as a garden under the care of the teacher. In his most influential work, the Great Didactic, he declares that the seeds of learning, virtue and religion are "naturally implanted in us."[1] The human mind, he says, is like a seed which, "if placed in the ground, puts forth roots beneath it and shoots above it, and these later on, by their own innate force, spread into branches and leaves, are covered with foliage, and adorned with flowers and fruit."[2]

---

1   Great Didactic, V, XIV. All quotations from the Great Didactic are taken from Keatinge, 1967.
2   Great Didactic V:5.

Comenius sees the school as a garden in which the task of the teacher is to "water God's plants."[3] Accordingly, he suggests that the different textbooks to be used in the different classes should have horticultural titles which "please and attract the young and ... at the same time express the nature of their contents." Thus, "the book of the lowest class might be called the violet-bed, that of the second class the rose-bed, that of the third class the grass-plot, and so on."[4] In keeping with this fondness for garden metaphors, Comenius urges as the overarching goal of education that each person is to become "a garden of delight for his God."[5]

Comenius' writings are important milestones in the history of education, and his richly metaphorical language helps to make them engaging and colourful. But how are his metaphorical habits relevant here, in the midst of a discussion of the Bible's relationship to education? This chapter will begin to explore the idea (pursued further in the two chapters which follow) that metaphors such as those used by Comenius can play a significant role in relating the Bible to education. Comenius' garden metaphors not only inform his educational thinking, they are also an important aspect of his attempt to think in the light of Scripture, as will become clearer below. Before looking at Comenius in more detail, however, it will be helpful to first get a more general sense of why metaphors might be important.

The relevance of metaphor

There has in recent decades been a marked shift in the prevailing view of metaphor. Until fairly recently the standard view saw metaphor as a poetic decoration designed to make language more colourful but at the same time less truthful and trustworthy.[6] On this view, metaphors

---

3   Great Didactic XVI:2.

4   Great Didactic XXIX:11. The suggestion is worked out further in the *Pampaedia* (*Pampaedia*, X in Dobbie, 1986), where the progression is amended and extended to the nursery garden, the seed bed, the violet bed, the rose garden, the shrubbery and the park.

5   Great Didactic, Dedicatory Letter.

6   This view emerged particularly from seventeenth century empiricism. See e.g. Soskice, 1985:1-14.

are like water lilies on a pond. They add to the beauty of the scene, but they must be skimmed away if we want to penetrate beyond the surface and find out what is going on in the depths below. The following extract from a discussion of language by philosopher John Wilson offers a forthright example of this kind of perspective:

> The beliefs of men, and perhaps particularly their religious beliefs, tend to seek expression in the most poetic form. The greatness of the Bible, for instance, lies not least in its high literary value. Prayers, political songs and slogans, proverbs and moral injunctions, and formalised ritual sayings of all kinds tend to acquire poetic force. This is desirable for many reasons, provided only that we do not lose sight of their prose meaning. Pure poetry is one thing; nobody 'takes it seriously'. Pure prose, such as a scientific text-book, is another; nobody feels inclined to read it in the sing-song, faintly mystical voice which we reserve for poetry. But mixed communications are dangerous, for we may easily allow their poetic force to blind us to the prose meaning … Prose communication consists of words of which we are intended to make logical sense: words which we are supposed to understand with our reason, not appreciate with our feelings. It is with this sort of communication that we shall be concerned, because this is the type of communication which we ought to use in arguing, discussing, solving problems and discovering truth.[7]

The implications of a view of metaphor as poetic decoration are clearly spelled out: if we are concerned with factual truth, we are urged to purge our language of such dubious appeals to the passions and stick to unadorned prose.[8] What is particularly interesting in the

---

7   Wilson, 1956:49-50.

8   Roger Lundin quotes the admonition from the seventeenth century British scientist Thomas Sprat that we should banish "Specious Tropes and Figures" from "all civil Societies as a thing fatal to Peace and good Manners", and that the Royal Society should adopt instead "a close, naked, natural way of speaking … as near the Mathematical plainness as they can" (Lundin, Walhout, & Thiselton, 1999:39)

present context is the explicit reference to the status of the Bible. Here again, the implications are clear. The fact that both religious language in general and the Bible in particular are laden with metaphor may be valuable in some way, we are told. We should, however, remember that if we want to find out the truth of the matter then the poetic images in the Bible must either be converted into cold prose or regarded as having no legitimate bearing on the facts. On this view, the metaphorical dimension of Scripture is likely to hinder rather than help in the task of relating it to education.

This view of metaphor is now widely regarded as untenable. Scholars in a wide variety of disciplines, including the natural sciences, have explored the essential role which metaphors play in our understanding of reality. Seeing electricity as a current or light as a wave or particle are not mere poetic aberrations, but a way of extending our knowledge by looking at one thing in terms of another.[9] Becoming accustomed to thinking in terms of a certain metaphor or group of metaphors can focus our attention in particular ways and guide us into certain patterns of practice.

A striking example of this is offered by Lakoff and Johnson in the opening pages of their book *Metaphors We Live By*.[10] They point out that in Western cultural contexts we tend to talk about argument as a form of warfare. We *attack* others' *positions* and *defend* or *buttress* our own. Our criticisms may be *on target* and if so may *demolish* or even *shoot down* an opposing argument. This, Lakoff and Johnson argue, is not merely poetic embellishment – it is the normal way for us to talk about arguing. It both reflects and helps to shape what we actually do when we argue.

In order to make the point clearer, they suggest that we should imagine a culture where argument is primarily viewed as a dance. We might then look at arguments more in terms of the ways in which the participants cooperate through turn-taking (a point obscured by warfare metaphors), and see the ideal as a poised performance which

---

9   See e.g. Lakoff & Johnson, 1980, 1999; Ortony, 1993; Sacks, 1979.
      Definitions of metaphor vary; for present purposes, the broad definition
      of metaphor offered by Soskice will suffice: "metaphor is that figure of
      speech whereby we speak about one thing in terms which are seen to be
      suggestive of another" (Soskice, 1985:15).

10   Lakoff & Johnson, 1980:3-6.

leaves both parties and any onlookers enriched and satisfied. The key point here is that while some metaphors may be one-off poetic images, others become much more deeply and pervasively embedded in our ways of thinking. They may shape both the way in which we see the world and the way in which we live in it.

Educational metaphors

To return to education, the metaphors which come to dominate our thinking about teaching and learning can have a significant impact on how we shape and experience education.[11] To take an example familiar in many Western contexts, once metaphors of economic production gain a hold on our perception of education, then those who lead schools become the *senior management team*, the curriculum becomes a *product* which we *deliver* to the children and parents who are its *consumers* and/or the school's *customers*, its delivery must be subjected to *quality control*, the school must *market* itself to parents and employers, and so on. The same metaphorical perspective can colour descriptions of the learning process itself, as in this example from an article on second language learning:

> "If learners invest in a second language, they do so with the understanding that they will acquire a wider range of symbolic and material resources, which will in turn increase the value of their cultural capital. Learners will expect or hope to have a good return on their investment – a return that will give them access to hitherto unattainable resources."[12]

Such networks of imagery are not merely a poetic way of describing what happens in schools – they both reflect and in turn help to create and sustain certain ways of doing and experiencing education.

---

11   On the importance of metaphor for education see e.g. the papers in Munby, 1986; Ortony, 1993; Taylor, 1984; Thornbury, 1991. On metaphor and Christian education see e.g. Shortt, Smith, & Cooling, 2000; Sullivan, 2000; Van Brummelen, 1992.

12   Peirce, 1995:17.

The realisation that metaphor is more than mere decoration calls for a re-evaluation of the role that it might play in relating the Bible to education. Educational discussion is inhabited and moulded by metaphors. Religious language and in particular the language of the Bible are richly metaphorical. Could there be a connection between the two? This question returns us to Comenius and his gardens.

Teaching as gardening

The image of the school as a garden in which the learners are little plants which will blossom and flourish if given space to thrive can readily be associated with child-centred education in the Romantic or progressive tradition stemming from Rousseau. This tradition commonly sees the learner as innately good and the civilising intervention of the teacher as a potentially damaging intrusion. It is typically contrasted with a more teacher-centred pedagogy, which tends to see learners as blank slates or empty receptacles to be written upon or filled with knowledge by the teacher. Comenius' talk of the innate seeds of learning watered by the teacher sounds close in spirit to the Romantic view.

As Daniel Murphy has recently argued, however, things are not that simple. Murphy notes that Comenius has often been seen as belonging to the progressive tradition, but he goes on to distinguish two strands of thought sharing broadly learner-centred ideals:

> The first of these strands includes educators such as Comenius himself, Oberlin, Pestalozzi, Froebel, Novikov, Pirogov, Tolstoy and Buber – all of whose works deeply reflect their origins in the cultural traditions of Christianity and Judaism. The second, which begins with Rousseau and reaches maturity with Dewey, stands in marked contrast to the first, by virtue of its advocacy of learner-centred ideals within the framework of a philosophy which is predominantly secular in character.[13]

---

13   Murphy, 1995:3.

How, then, does this deep difference in the relationship of these educators' ideas to Christian belief become evident? In the case of Comenius, the use to which he puts his gardening metaphors provides an interesting avenue of investigation.

At times, Comenius does sound very close to Rousseau. The imagery of naturally implanted seeds of virtue, and of education as organic growth, echo common progressive themes. The modern reader who is led by this imagery to expect an earlier version of Rousseau is, however, in for some puzzlement, for Comenius is happy on other occasions to view the school as a workshop, education as the operation of a printing press imprinting knowledge upon the learner, or the human person as a clock.[14] He also presents the teacher not only as one who is to "open the fountain of knowledge that is hidden in the scholars", but also as one whose mouth is "a spring from which streams of knowledge issue and flow over them" or who, like the sun, should be the centre of attention.[15] This sounds much less like the child-centred classroom. Was Comenius just confused? Closer attention to the contexts that inform his imagery suggests that this would be a premature conclusion.

Interpreting the garden of delights

First, it is helpful to consider the *experiential* context of his garden metaphors. A few years ago, a visit to a medieval stately home in

---

14   The machine images seem to evoke for Comenius, standing at the dawn of modernity, a sense of wonder rather than more jaded present-day perceptions of determinism, deism or disenchantment. The vision is not of rigid structure but of a harmonious movement together of all the parts, whether limbs or levers. Cf. *Great Didactic* XIII:14 : "If any part get out of position, crack, break, become loose or bent, though it be the smallest wheel, the most insignificant axle, or the tiniest screw, the whole machine stops or at least goes wrong, and thus shows us plainly that everything depends on the harmonious working of the parts." Schaller (1992:24) argues that for Comenius the machine metaphor represents "alles, was … für den unkundigen Zuschauer verblüffende Wirkungen zeigt." (everything which shows astonishing operations to the unknowledgable onlooker).

15   *Great Didactic* XVIII:23, XIX:19, 20.

Derbyshire, England, made the contours of Comenius' image visually vivid. The route laid out for visitors led through the house and out into a very beautiful and carefully patterned flower garden. On one side of the garden was a path edged by a low wall, offering views of rolling open countryside beyond the garden's boundaries. The contrast with the modern urban experience of gardening was striking. To the modern city dweller, a garden is a small intrusion of nature in the territory of culture, a vulnerable patch of green offering relief from the overwhelming dominance of human artefacts, a clearing in the concrete jungle. At this historic country house the garden was, as for Comenius, an island of culture in the sea of nature, a place where disciplined beauty was brought forth from the unruliness of nature. With the garden metaphor as with many other metaphors, including those in Scripture, apt personal experience plays an important role in interpretation.

Second, the garden metaphor has a developed *theological* context in Comenius' writings, a point that becomes evident if we consider his understanding of 'nature'. Comenius states that:

> "by the word nature we mean, not the corruption which has laid hold of all men since the Fall (on which account we are naturally called the children of wrath, unable by ourselves to have any good thoughts), but our first and original condition, to which as a starting-point we must be recalled."[16]

Talk of human 'nature' does not refer simply to the way things are, to humans as we find them around us, but to the good creation, now distorted by the Fall, but recoverable through the processes of redemption. The world should by rights be a garden, but has become a wilderness. God's work through 'natural' agencies such as education is, in Comenius' view, to play a significant role in the process of renewal.

Moreover, even apart from the distorting effects of sin, human 'nature' is not a given thing, completed and self-sufficient, but rather a "starting-point" for a process of development which is to continue throughout this life and into the next![7] Human 'nature' is not a

---

16   *Great Didactic* V:1.

17   *Great Didactic* II:5.

possession already within our grasp – it is a calling from which we have stumbled and which must be progressively recovered and realised. It will only be attained "in full plenitude" in the presence of God in eternity.[18] Once we see how Comenius understands 'nature', it becomes clear that to compare the development of the child with the 'natural' growth of a seed does not discourage the teacher's formative intervention – it *invites* it. As Comenius points out, "Herbs and grains have to be sown, hoed and ground; trees have to be planted, pruned and manured, while their fruits must be plucked off and dried; and if any of these things are required for medicine, or for building purposes, much more preparation is needed."[19]

Leaving 'natural' processes unattended is not a benevolent but an irresponsible course of action: just as "a wild tree will not bring forth sweet fruits until it be planted, watered and pruned by a skilled gardener, so does a man grow of his own accord into a human semblance (just as any brute resembles others of his own class), but is unable to develope into a rational, wise, virtuous and pious creature, unless virtue and piety are first engrafted in him."[20] A garden is not a refuge from civilisation but rather something to be shaped in God-pleasing ways by a wise and careful gardener.[21] Again we find that the garden

---

18   *Great Didactic* II:10.

19   *Great Didactic* VI:3.

20   *Great Didactic* VII:1. Comenius cites examples of children who were raised by wild animals and whose human faculties remained undeveloped (*Great Didactic* VI:6). Cf. *Pampaedia* II:3: "nature should not be allowed to lie neglected and contribute neither to the glory of God nor to man's salvation." Cicero's statement that "the seeds of virtue are sown in our dispositions, and, if they are allowed to develope, nature herself would lead us to the life of the blest" is explicitly rejected – not because such seeds are not present but because something more than nature is needed to bring them to fruition (*Great Didactic* V:13). Contrast Rousseau's complaint that "Man ... not content to leave anything as nature has made it, ... must needs shape man himself to his notions, as he does the trees in his garden" and his admonition "Do you not see that in attempting to improve on [nature's] work you are destroying it and defeating the provision she has made?" (Boyd, 1956:11,17).

21   *Great Didactic* XVI:2. Cf. *Pampaedia* I:15.

for Comenius is not an image of unspoiled nature, but rather of nature carefully brought under discipline that it might bear greater fruit.[22]

Third, the garden metaphors in Comenius' writings are explicitly rooted in the text of the Bible. The opening chapters of the *Great Didactic* are devoted to an exposition of what it means to be created in the image of God, a significant theme of the opening chapter of Genesis. According to Comenius, this includes lordship over creation, understood not as exploitative mastery but as service. True lordship is a wise tending of the garden and involves working to bring all things to their proper fruition so that "all creatures should have cause to join us in praising God".[23] The opening chapters of Genesis come even more explicitly to the fore in the dedicatory letter, which opens with a description of the original paradise:

> God, having created man out of dust, placed him in a Paradise of desire, which he had planted in the East, not only that man might tend it and care for it, but also that he might be a garden of delight for his God.

Humankind is not just to tend a garden, but to *be* a garden. After a description of the delights of Paradise, the "pleasantest part of the world" in which "each tree was delightful to look at," Comenius reiterates that "each man is, in truth, a Garden of Delights for his God, as long as he remains in the spot where he has been placed". He goes on to state that the church, too, "is often in Holy Writ likened to a Paradise, to a garden, to a vineyard of God".[24] Hovering behind Comenius'

---

22   See e.g. *Great Didactic* XVI:48; also (Schaller, 1992:24): a garden for Comenius is to be read as "nicht Natur, sondern gestaltete Natur" – not nature but nature given form.

23   *Pampaedia* II:13. Cf. *Great Didactic* IV:4: "To be the lord of all creatures consists in subjecting everything to his own use by contriving that its legitimate end be suitably fulfilled; in conducting himself royally, that is gravely and righteously, among creatures … [not being] ignorant where, when, how and to what extent each may prudently be used, how far the body should be gratified, and how far our neighbour's interests should be consulted. In a word, he should be able to control with prudence his own movements and actions, external and internal, as well as those of others."

garden imagery is the garden of Eden as described in Genesis chapters 1-3, and in its train the whole subsequent network of garden and vineyard imagery in the Bible. For Comenius, the garden images are not just homely comparisons; they are a way of drawing the imagery of Scripture into his account of education.

Metaphor, the Bible and education

In Comenius we see a biblical metaphor playing a formative role in educational thinking. Comenius was not the only educator to see the educational context as a garden, but his use of garden metaphors is rooted in a biblical image of gardening – to be specific, in the Bible's representation of the garden of Eden. His talk of gardens therefore evokes not merely natural growth but the biblical drama of creation, fall and redemption. Through the conscious echoes of Eden, the garden metaphor evokes themes of God's pleasure and displeasure, of human calling and responsibility, of failure and guilt, and of redemptive re-formation.

It is against this background that the garden of delights becomes a fertile image for Comenius, helping him to develop and articulate a particular vision of schooling. Gardens are seen as places of disciplined cultivation leading to fruitfulness and to shared divine and human pleasure. The learning process must accordingly be both ordered and enjoyable, involving both discipline (cultivation) and playfulness (delight). A high view of learners and of the potential which God has placed in them is coupled with a strong sense of the teacher's responsibility to 'plant, water and prune.' These are the contours within which Comenius' more detailed proposals unfold.[25] The garden image both plays a role in shaping Comenius' ideas and helps him to capture his readers' imaginations, enticing and enabling them to see education as he saw it.

The garden imagery resonates with a particular theology, but it is not replaceable without loss by any single doctrinal formulation. In his talk of schools as gardens of delight, Comenius offers us not a set of

---

24   *Great Didactic*, Dedicatory letter.

25   A detailed exposition of Comenius' pedagogy would be out of place here. For further detail, see Smith, 2000b.

premises or propositions from which to make deductions, but rather an image to think with, something to set our imaginations going along biblically oriented lines. The image alone, bereft of its theological context, could carry a variety of contradictory meanings, Christian or otherwise. The image taken in context plays a significant role in Comenius' attempt to think about education in the light of Scripture.

In this chapter we have tried to illustrate how metaphors can forge connections between the Bible and education. In the next two chapters we will explore this kind of process in more detail, attending first to the ways in which individual images get taken up into wider networks of meaning and then to the benefits and problems which flow from the tendency of metaphor to be open to a variety of interpretations.

10

What is a biblical metaphor?

What makes a metaphor 'biblical'?

The manner in which Comenius marshalled his horticultural images reflects the pervasive influence of the Bible in his educational writings. Given the common tendency to think of the Bible's relationship to education in terms of making inferences from biblical principles or propositions, this feature of Comenius' writing is of more than historical interest, for it suggests a different approach. However, important questions remain. Can we simply regard the Bible as a quarry from which we can extract educational metaphors at will? Is it legitimate to take any image from the Bible and spin educational ideas out of it? What does it mean for an educational metaphor to be 'biblical'?

Just borrowing?

The simplest and most obvious answer is to say that a 'biblical meta-phor' is 'one which is taken from the Bible'. In other words, if we take an image found in Scripture and find an educational use for it, then we are using a biblical metaphor. This seems to fit what we saw in Comenius – he took the pregnant image of the garden of paradise from the pages of the Bible and put it to educational use.

While this answer may be simple, obvious and appealing, it will not do, for at least three reasons. First, the Bible takes its images and meta-phors from human experience. There seems to be no reason to suppose that the images found in the Bible are in themselves specially *authorised* as images, apart from the particular use to which they are put in Scripture. The fact that imagery involving rocks, mother hens, trees, winepresses, sheep and the like is copiously present in Scripture does not at all imply that the use of similar imagery in relation to, say, a chemistry course is necessarily in any way 'biblical'. In the Bible God is described as a fortress – but there seems little reason to suppose that thinking of the school teacher as a fortress would be a particularly 'biblical' thing to do. What carries authority is a particular use of the fortress image to talk about God, not the image in itself or its potential use in other contexts.

Second, since the imagery of the Bible is not *unique*, an image found in educational reflection may also appear in the Bible but this may be coincidence; it may not have significant biblical roots. In its educational context the image may express meanings quite foreign to the biblical text. We have already seen an example of this in the contrast between Comenius' and Rousseau's use of horticultural imagery, where similar imagery is used to present significantly differ-ent visions of education. We could cull an image from the Bible and apply it to all kinds of things, but the connection with the Bible's understanding of the world may be tenuous at best.

Third, harvesting imagery at will from the Bible may not be partic-ularly *helpful*. The fruitfulness of a metaphor in one context is no guarantee that it will be illuminating in a different context. A meta-phor which works powerfully in communicating a sense of how we should view some aspect of salvation may turn out to stimulate no particularly helpful lines of thought if we try to use it as a way of seeing, say, a school timetable.

In sum, if we think merely in terms of borrowing imagery, the Bible may (like any other fertile and evocative text) be a source of ideas, and those ideas might or might not prove helpful in educational terms, but it is not clear that the results would be 'biblical' in any strong sense simply by virtue of their incidental source. What we have in mind here is not, then, simply taking an image from the Bible and transferring it into an educational discussion. This first answer, despite its initial appeal, will not suffice.

Worldview critique?

A different answer to the question of how an educational metaphor could be biblical points not simply to the imagery itself, but to its cognitive claims. Harro Van Brummelen, in an article that offers a Christian critique of some prominent educational metaphors, suggests that "most educational metaphors are rooted in or imply a concept of human beings and their world".[1] Metaphors implicitly embody claims about the way things are. These claims may be consonant with or in tension with a Christian understanding of the world. Seeing persons as machines, for instance, conveys reductive messages that do not sit comfortably with an emphasis on persons being made in God's image. Given that Christian educators, like all educators, cannot avoid working with particular metaphors for various aspects of teaching and learning, "we need to work with ones that reflect our beliefs and our aims".[2] Our Christian worldview should guide and regulate our dealings with metaphor just as it should guide and regulate our other dealings in the world.

This second suggestion seems more promising than the first. Like the first, it appears to be applicable to the discussion of Comenius in the previous chapter. The discussion there focussed not only on the garden image taken purely as an image, but also on its consistency with a worldview in which the themes of creation, divine-human fellowship and human responsibility played a key role. Instead of just borrowing images from the Bible, this approach wants to examine all images, from whatever source, for their implied worldview as it

---

1   Van Brummelen, 1992:170.
2   Van Brummelen, 1992:170.

emerges in the context of particular uses.

This process of scrutinising imagery in the light of Christian belief is indeed valuable, and many attempts to think Christianly about education are likely to proceed along these lines, identifying the basic images which drive an educational approach and subjecting them to scrutiny in the light of a Christian worldview. While valuable, however, this way of understanding the role of metaphors in Christian educational thinking is not the whole story.

Its weakness, as far as the present discussion is concerned, is opposite to that of the first answer. The first answer had the merit of focusing on the use of images taken directly from the Bible, but it raised the problem that the new use of the borrowed image may not be very 'biblical'. This second answer asks us to evaluate our metaphors in the light of a biblical worldview, but is less directly concerned with the role that might be played by the imagery found in the Bible itself. Van Brummelen explores the potential not only of viewing learners as images of God and teaching as a religious craft, but also of seeing the curriculum as a route map or an amoeba. The metaphors discussed are potential aids to educational reflection, and can come from any source, not just the Bible. The process of evaluation involves stating their implied worldview and then matching it up with the Bible's worldview. In other words, our metaphors become one more thing to be matched up with our conceptually articulated biblical worldview. This matching process is valuable, but it seems to be another instance of the approach discussed in chapter 5, where the Bible is related to education by working out the implications of a more propositionally stated worldview.

What is not sufficiently explored here is the possibility that metaphor itself might shape and inform our worldview, rather than being that which our worldview examines. If our basic metaphors actually shape our worldview, then perhaps the metaphors themselves provide a more direct link between the Bible and education.

What do metaphors evoke?

If these two answers are both incomplete, the question remains: what do we mean here by educational metaphors being 'biblical'? In order to develop a more adequate answer we need to return to recent discussions of how fertile metaphors work.

It is commonly pointed out that a fertile metaphor does not simply compare two things at a single point, but rather gives rise to an open-ended series of resonances, so that the task of listing what the metaphor means becomes almost boundless. The simple phrase "the Lord is my shepherd" is not adequately translated by any single statement such as "the Lord will protect me", "the Lord will see that I am fed" or "the Lord will show me which way to go". It implies any or all of these and many more besides: the Lord has an interest in my welfare, the Lord is stronger and wiser than I, I am part of a flock, I can't see enough of the road ahead for myself ... meditation on the verse could extend the list considerably. When we respond to this metaphor, we are not confined to a single characteristic of shepherd; we draw upon a whole range of facets of the relationship between shepherds and sheep. It is this process which makes the replacement of a fertile metaphor by a literal equivalent so inadequate.[3]

The list becomes longer once it is noted that personal experience comes into play. A metaphor does not merely evoke the defining properties of the things referred to, properties which could be assumed to be the same for everyone. A reader's or hearer's response to an arresting metaphor will typically also include a variety of more personal reminiscences and associations. When I think of the tree of life, my mind is drawn not only to the general properties of trees, but to the tree which grows in a neighbour's garden and is visible from my kitchen window. In particular I find myself picturing the way in which, early on a breezy summer evening, the rays of the setting sun reflected from the myriad rapidly moving leaves can turn the tree into a mass of exuberant vitality. My response to a metaphor draws both upon the more general properties of that which is imaged (shepherds, sheep, trees) and upon my own more personal experiences.[4]

There is one more crucial element. When Gerard Manley Hopkins, referring to his mortality and the hope of resurrection, writes "Across my foundering deck shone/ A beacon, an eternal beam",[5] I personally find the metaphor evocative, but its meaning for me does not derive from my first-hand experience. I do not think of the ships on which I

---

3   Cf. Black, 1993; Davidson, 1979.

4   Of course, the difference between metaphor and non-metaphorical language on this point may be only one of degree.

5   Hopkins, 1970:105.

have travelled, for none of them have (at least while I was on them) foundered or been illuminated by a lighthouse. I do not think of the ships of my own day, or even of Hopkins' day. Instead, I find myself thinking of the sailing ships of old and of images drawn from films, novels and biographies that I have seen and read, from Robert Louis Stevenson's *Kidnapped*, Defoe's *Robinson Crusoe*, or John Newton's life story. Others may, of course, respond differently, but the point is that a metaphor can evoke not just my experience of the world, but my experience of *other texts*.

What's more, as metaphor shades into literary allusion, the pointers can be to a specific story. If someone comments regarding a mutual friend "he's a real Sherlock Holmes", my attention is drawn to the qualities of a particular character in a particular narrative. The passing reference provides a point of contact which opens out into a specific, bounded set of stories and the images of acumen and incisive reasoning which they contain. Those stories and images become the filter through which I am invited to view my friend, perhaps seeing him in an entirely new light as a result.

Towards a more robust answer

We are now in a position to glimpse a more robust sense in which an educational metaphor might be biblical. Metaphors can generate a widening field of perceptions, enabling us to see and do things in new ways. They appeal not only to our knowledge of the typical properties of the things referred to, but also to our experience. This experience may be first-hand personal experience, or it may be our acquaintance with particular texts, ideas and stories. The sense in which Comenius' garden metaphors were biblical rests on all of these points. The garden imagery was designed to connect the reader's experience both of gardens and of children with a particular biblical narrative. It formed the point of contact, the bridge connecting the story of Eden and its particular theological perspective with the reader's experience and educational realities. Metaphor can function to evoke a specifically biblical set of resonances.

This expands our earlier answers. In a loose sense, as we have seen, a metaphor might be described as biblical if the view of the world which it invites is consistent with that found in the Bible. In a stricter sense, what we have in mind when we refer to a biblical metaphor is one which *is drawn from the Bible and which mediates the distinctive web of meanings found in the biblical text into a new situation*. This is more than just extracting an image at random and reapplying it without regard for the network of meaning from which it was extracted. The warrant for using a biblical metaphor in this stronger sense is not that the image happens to occur in Scripture, but that it draws us into the wisdom of Scripture.

Clearly, a metaphor which is biblical in this stronger sense will be consistent with the beliefs reflected in the Bible, but the process is not simply one of lining practices up with beliefs. It is the metaphor itself which provides the point of contact with Scripture and which sets up an open-ended set of interactions between biblical images, stories and ideas and educational practices. The process of thinking about education in the light of a theologically pregnant image must bring beliefs into play. It is, however, a different process from that of working out the consequences of more propositionally stated beliefs. Metaphor can join faith to practice through the medium of imagination.[6]

So what?

As we noted in the last chapter, when metaphors begin to resonate with our experience they can lead to pervasive shifts in our practice. A fertile metaphor applied to some aspect of our practice can generate a variety of fresh perceptions, some of which may suggest new ways of doing things. As Donald Schön relates, even such an apparently technical process as designing a paintbrush can be redirected through a shift in the designer's mental image. A group of designers had, Schön reports, been trying in vain to design a paintbrush with synthetic bristles which would paint as smoothly as one made from natural fibres. They had varied the properties of the new bristles without success, until someone remarked that a paintbrush is basically a pump. This shifted their attention away from the way in which the brush wiped paint onto surfaces. They began to think of the brush instead in terms of the action of a pump, pumping paint out onto the surfaces. Examining the way in which the paint was pushed through the hollow

---

6   Cf. Harris, 1987.

spaces between the bristles led to a successful design.[7]

In education more is at stake than technique. Educational discussion is always in some measure discussion about how we *should* educate – how we should treat children, what kind of communities we should create, what aspirations we should affirm, what goals we should set. Educational inquiry cannot be reduced to a clinical matter of determining the most efficient techniques; it inevitably involves normative considerations. A change of image can impact even such a technical matter as designing a paintbrush; the corresponding shifts which a change of image can bring about in educational practice are much more far-reaching. In this arena, it makes an enormous difference how we see. Metaphors encode the expectations which we have of the educational process. They also communicate those expectations to others and give them a sense of what they can expect from the educational institution.[8] They play an important role in shaping and expressing our basic vision. If metaphors are not water lilies on a pond, decorative and opaque, but can instead be windows through which the light of a particular vision of reality is refracted, then an exploration of how metaphors can refract a biblical vision is surely of considerable significance to Christian educators.

Roots and clusters

Our discussion so far already suggests ways in which particular metaphors can function to bring parts of the biblical story into interaction with educational thought and practice. One important limitation of what we have said is that we have been focusing on individual metaphors. Many studies of metaphor have pointed out that the metaphors which inhabit our thinking tend to form clusters or networks loosely organised around a particular root metaphor.[9] This tendency showed in the examples discussed in the last chapter. The root image of the school as a site of economic production was at the heart of a wider pattern of imagery including learners as investors, knowledge as capital, assessment as quality control, and so on. The basic image of arguing as

---

7   Schön, 1993.
8   See Beavis & Thomas, 1996.
9   Ricœur, 1981.

warfare connects a variety of expressions such as shooting down, defending or buttressing arguments. Comenius' vision of teaching as gardening was at the heart of a network of imagery which included learners as plants, teaching as watering, learning as fruit-bearing, books as flower beds, and so on.

These wider networks of imagery help both to develop and to constrain the meaning of the basic image. They develop it in that they extend its reach, hooking it up to various more specific aspects of whatever is being described. They constrain it in that they give a more extensively sketched out shape to a basic image which might otherwise be developed in a different direction.

Love and power

We will consider another biblically-derived example of this clustering of metaphors in educational discussion, starting from Parker Palmer's book *To know as we are known: A spirituality of education*.[10] Palmer's basic argument is that Western education has suffered from a view of knowledge as power. We wrestle with issues, try to master or penetrate areas of learning, manipulate ideas, crack problems and hammer out solutions. Such a view of knowledge, Palmer argues, encourages and sustains a stance towards learning in which we approach the world as simply an object to be dissected, manipulated and mastered. We end up focused on forcing reality to submit to our perceived needs and prying into secrets which will give us more mastery over life. "Curiosity and control are joined as the passion behind our knowing."[11]

Palmer argues that we should question our understanding of knowing as power, for

> another kind of knowledge is available to us, one that begins in a different passion and is drawn toward other ends ... This is a knowledge that originates not in curiosity or control but in compassion, or love – a source celebrated not in our intellectual tradition but in our spiritual heritage.[12]

10   Palmer, 1983.
11   Palmer, 1983:7.
12   Palmer, 1983:8.

He argues that we need to recover "from our spiritual tradition the models and methods of knowing as an act of love", claiming that "the act of knowing is an act of love, the act of entering and embracing the reality of the other, of allowing the other to enter and embrace our own."[13]

He is careful to specify what kind of love he has in mind. This love is "not a soft and sentimental virtue, not a fuzzy feeling of romance" but rather "the connective tissue of reality" which calls us to "involvement, mutuality, accountability".[14] In fact, Palmer has a specific model in mind. He appeals to Paul's description of love in 1 Corinthians chapter 13, thus couching his proposal in specifically biblical terms.[15]

Whether Palmer's basic claim that knowing is loving is intended as a proposal that we should adopt a different metaphor for knowing or as a more literal claim, what he says invites us to shift the wider pattern of imagery which we associate with knowing, learning and teaching. Palmer maps this shift further in the remainder of his book, but here we will turn to some other Christian writings on education which can be seen as contributing to the same pattern or cluster.

In a brief article published earlier than Palmer's book, Brian Hill argued that:

> Teaching style is not just a matter of possessing certain skills, but of seeing the teaching situation in its wholeness. We depend on models and metaphors to bind together the bits of experience ... (M)any dimensions of the teacher's task can be woven together by the biblical concept of reconciliation.[16]

Hill writes that reconciliation should be understood here in a way which leans heavily on Scripture. It refers in its biblical context to God's ending, on his initiative and at great cost to himself, of the enmity towards him caused by our rebellion. It should lead Christians into a ministry of reconciliation, and Hill suggests that one way of relating this to education is to apply the biblical idea of reconciliation metaphorically to areas of educational thought and practice where

---

13   Palmer, 1983:8-9.
14   Palmer, 1983:9.
15   Palmer, 1983:15.
16   Hill, 1976:15.

things are out of joint. He refers specifically to tensions between the child and society, oppositions between thinking and feeling, and conflicts between different groups in the making of educational policy. Teachers, he suggests, should see their involvement in education as a metaphorical extension of God's great act of reconciliation.

A further example can be found in a recent book about foreign language education. David Smith and Barbara Carvill explore the implications of seeing foreign language learning as a form of hospitality to the stranger.[17] Their discussion draws upon the biblical call to "love the alien as yourself".[18] The aim is, however, not to claim that this biblical injunction intended to address pedagogical issues in present day foreign language education. The aim is rather to ask how those issues look if we adopt hospitality to the stranger as our basic image for foreign language learning. This might on occasion mean literally hosting members of the culture being studied; most often, however, it will refer metaphorically to how we interact with the foreign language and culture as we learn, inviting it into our personal space and interacting with it graciously.[19] This image turns out to have a variety of consequences for the aims, content and methods of the foreign language curriculum, shifting the focus away from the rehearsal of consumer transactions and towards a more central interest in the lives and stories of members of the other culture.

Theological patterns

If we draw these three examples together, we find them forming an interrelated pattern. Palmer says that we should think of knowing as loving and explore the implications of that image for how we view teaching and learning. Hill's argument can be seen as addressing the question of how this is affected by the divisions and enmities of the educational world as we find it. Smith and Carvill ask: given that the basic human call is to love God and to love our neighbour, what kind of love is particularly relevant to encountering and learning about those from other languages and cultures?

---

17   Smith & Carvill, 2000; see also Carvill, 1991a, 1991b.

18   See e.g. Leviticus 19:34-35.

19   Smith & Carvill, 2000:83-103.

Moving beyond individual instances of biblical metaphors being given a role in educational reflection, to a consideration of how they link up into coherent networks, both helps to give them more specific meaning and extends their reach into various more specific aspects of education. Moreover, the connections among the different images mirror a biblical pattern. In the Bible, love of God and love of one's neighbour are placed centre-stage, reconciliation when these relationships stand broken is the heart of the Gospel, and love for strangers is repeatedly put forward as a specific form of love for one's neighbour.[20] The educational examples outlined above reflect not only individual biblical images, but also the pattern of relationships within the Bible between the centrality of love, the fallenness of the world and our relationships to strangers. Again we find that educational imagery can be the vehicle through which the Bible's influence becomes manifest.

Much more could be said in terms of a detailed appraisal of the examples offered here. For present purposes, however, the main concern is to clarify and illustrate how the Bible can interact with education through its *imagery* becoming interwoven with our educational vision. As David Tracy puts it,

> not only is every major religion grounded in certain root metaphors, but Western religions are also 'religions of the book' – books which codify root metaphors ... For Judaism, Christianity, and Islam certain texts serve not only as charter documents for the religion, but as 'scripture' in the strict sense: that is as normative for the religious community's basic understanding and control of its root metaphors and thereby its vision of reality.[21]

In other words, our most basic metaphors do not just sit there waiting to be evaluated by our worldview; they *mould* our worldview.

---

20   See e.g. Leviticus 19:18, 34-35; Matthew 25:34-36; Luke 10:25-37.
21   Tracy, 1979:90.

11

Weeding the garden

The last two chapters have dwelt largely on the positive possibilities of relating the Bible to education through the medium of metaphor. What about the downside? If we move away from propositionally expressed doctrine into the slippery world of image and metaphor, will we find educational responses to the Bible becoming overly subjective? If fertile metaphors evoke an open-ended, expanding set of meanings, are there any boundaries? If metaphors can mean different things to different people, if botanical imagery can mean one thing to Comenius and another thing to Rousseau, are there any limits to the meanings which we can spin out of an image drawn from Scripture? Even though it could be retorted here that a focus on propositions has hardly prevented disagreements over interpretation or a variety of subjective responses, will an emphasis on metaphor not simply make matters worse? When we examine the relationships between propositions, there are at least familiar standards of logical coherence and consistency which can be applied – how can we judge the biblical faithfulness of metaphorical reflection?

What is an *un*biblical metaphor?

Our exploration in the last chapter of what might responsibly be understood as a 'biblical' educational metaphor helps to point us towards some answers to these questions. There we emphasised that what we have in mind is not simply a random borrowing of imagery from Scripture, but rather a process in which the metaphor both informs educational thinking and remains embedded in a theological context. That context sets broad limits to its interpretation.

Biblically allusive metaphors presume some familiarity on the recipient's part with their wider Scriptural background. Comenius assumes that we are familiar with the Genesis narrative, which should condition how we understand his garden metaphors. Palmer, perhaps feeling able to assume less on the part of his readers, feels it necessary to explain the specific idea of love which he has in mind by discussing 1 Corinthians chapter 13. A biblical metaphor, in the sense developed here, draws its background biblical texts into the process of its interpretation.

Another relevant part of the theological context is provided by wider networks of imagery. Within Scripture, for instance, the image of God as a shepherd could, if taken in isolation, be taken to imply that God is shabby, poor, unwashed and worthy of little respect. These aspects of the image are excluded partly by the immediate context of the image and partly by a wider pattern of imagery in which God is also referred to as a lord and a king. The wider network of images helps to condition the interpretation of any single image. Here again, responsibly tracing the biblical sense of an image or metaphor will involve attending to wider contexts of meaning.

If the way in which an image is developed in educational thinking leads to tensions with this wider biblical context, then we can conclude that the image has not been entirely successful in relating the Bible to education. We will consider an example in more detail.

In the late 1960s and early 1970s Charles A. Curran developed an approach to education which he called "Counseling-learning".[1]

---

1   Curran, 1972, 1976.

It was based on the client-centred approach to counselling, which was developed by figures such as Carl Rogers under the broad umbrella of humanistic psychology. This movement in psychology emphasised the individual's existential experience and inherent potential for personal growth if freed from outside control.[2] Curran's pedagogy echoed these emphases. He demanded that the teacher withdraw from the central position of authority in the classroom and allow learners to direct the pace and content of lessons. The teacher was to provide warm and carefully uncritical support when invited to do so by the students.[3]

The interesting point here is that Curran explicitly claimed that his approach to education was consistent with a Judeo-Christian view of the person.[4] In fact he went further than this and introduced terms drawn from Christian theology directly into his theory of learning, describing learning as an "incarnate-redemptive process". He did not intend these terms to be taken straightforwardly in their theological sense,[5] but argued that there is a "parallel or correspondence" between religious realities and psychological processes. This parallel, he argued, means that the imagery of incarnation, redemption, rebirth and dying to self can be illuminating in relation to educational psychology.[6]

Curran used a whole network of theological metaphors to expound his theory of learning. For present purposes we will home in on his use of the term "incarnation". He used the term in two related senses.

---

2   See e.g. May, 1969.

3   For the details see Curran, 1972, 1976.

4   Curran saw his proposals as rooted in the "Judeo-Greco-Christian tradition of the view of man and of the human encounter as something engaging him in his whole, existent and corporeal person" (Curran, 1972:49).

5   Oller (Oller & Richard-Amato, 1983) criticised Curran for suggesting that the teacher could replace God as the one who redeems; Curran's rhetoric can at times invite that impression, but he also noted that the sense in which he was using the language of incarnation and redemption was distinct from, and not intended to replace, theological usage (see e.g. Curran, 1969:192, and the discussion in Stevick, 1990:77-96)

6   Curran, 1969:175.

'Incarnation' for the learner

On the one hand, he wrote of the need for the *learner* to become 'incarnate'. He wanted to resist the tendency in Western thought to detach the intellect from the body and the emotions. In its place he wanted to develop a view of learning which addressed the 'whole person'. Following Jean-Paul Sartre, he suggested that the basic human condition is that of wanting to be God, resisting our sense of finitude and grasping for power over others and our environment.[7] In our desire to forget our finitude, Curran argued, we tend to distance ourselves from the concrete emotional and bodily aspects of personhood and take refuge in intellectualised abstraction. We cling to the security of what we know, favouring abstract concepts that seem to take us beyond our bodily limitations. As a consequence, we become resistant to the new learning that comes through full-bodied immersion in communal life with others – it is easier to play God when one is alone. Thus, Curran argued, we become divided against ourselves (intellect versus feelings) and confined within ourselves (closed to others). If this state of affairs is to be overcome, if our whole person is to become engaged in learning, then we need to learn to accept ourselves. We need to become one with our body and feelings and leave the world of detached abstraction for the world of warm and open engagement. This is one sense in which Curran uses the language of incarnation – the detached 'I' must die to its ambitions and become 'incarnate', that is, must become one with the concrete, feeling self.[8]

'Incarnation' for the teacher

The second sense of 'incarnation' for Curran had to do with the relationship between the *teacher* and the group of learners. To the beginning learner, the teacher is god-like – an omniscient judge who has absolute command of the material being studied and who rules sovereignly over what goes on in the classroom. This presents temptations to both teacher and learners. The teacher may be tempted to live out his or her desire to be God by maintaining distance from the learners

---

7   Sartre, 1957:63; Curran, 1972:64-67.
8   E.g. Curran, 1972:19, 67, 98.

and dominating them, filling the learning space with his or her own authoritative words. The learners, due to their own desire to be God, may under such circumstances become resistant to learning from the teacher and alienated from the learning process. The teacher, Curran argues, must take the initiative in bringing redemption into the situation. He or she must overcome this enmity by leaving his or her God-like position. The teacher must die to self by giving up the position of dominance and joining the learners in their vulnerable state. The teacher becomes a fellow member of the learning group, and Curran saw this as implying that he or she must yield control over the curriculum to the learners, adopt a supportive role, and accept the criticisms of learners without resistance or self-defence. This change in role on the teacher's part is the second sense which Curran gives to the term 'incarnation'.[9]

'Incarnation' and its problems

Curran's use of incarnational language is interesting and suggestive. It is not hard to see how the image of incarnation, used metaphorically, could awaken associations of self-sacrificial humility for the Christian teacher. After all, the New Testament urges that "your attitude should be the same as that of Christ Jesus: who being in very nature God, did not consider equality with God something to be grasped, but made himself nothing."[10] We saw in chapter 7 that this passage may well be intended as a contrast to Adam's grasping after equality with God. Instead of such grasping it invites us to the same humility that Christ showed in the incarnation. It could lead our imaginations further still, as Curran saw, to a parallel between the dignifying of human flesh through Christ's incarnation and the teacher raising the dignity of the learners by taking a humble position in their midst. There is, then, a positive Christian rationale behind Curran's use of the image of incarnation.

It is, however, not without its difficulties. The passage from Philippians just quoted notes how Jesus "made himself nothing, taking on the very nature of a servant" and "humbled himself and became

---

9   E.g. Curran, 1972:31.

10   Philippians 2:6-7.

obedient to death". The emphasis here is on the depth of Christ's descent from the glory that was his by right, the marvel of his conde-scension in taking on the weakness of human nature. If we look closely at Curran's use of the term 'incarnation' we find a mismatch at this point.

Take the first meaning of 'incarnation'. Curran is here trying to describe a move away from an overly intellectualised and disembod-ied view of the self. The 'disincarnate' state is one of intellectual abstraction, emotional detachment and self-enclosed isolation from others. It is a deficient state. Becoming 'incarnate' means becoming *more* real, *more* concrete, *more* open and involved. But in the biblical story which Curran is evoking, this picture does not fit. To make it fit we would need to view God prior to the incarnation as distant, cold and uninvolved, a far cry from the passionately engaged God depicted in the pages of the Old Testament. We would also need to view the incarnation as a matter of this detached, abstract, self-enclosed God becoming *more real* by taking on flesh. This is not the sense conveyed by the verses we considered from Philippians chapter 2. 'Incarnation' for Curran does involve a certain kind of humbling of oneself, and a rejection of grasping after equality with God, but ultimately it is seen as a process of becoming *more whole*, and this does not echo well the biblical emphasis on a deeply involved God condescending out of mercy to take on the *less* substantial frailty of flesh.[11]

There are similar difficulties with Curran's second usage. If what is emphasised here is the teacher's humility and care for the learners, and his or her refusal to grasp after potential privilege in order to take up a position of vulnerable service, then this second usage does have some biblical substance. It may authentically communicate a call to have the same attitude as Christ, taking up the role of one who serves. However, Curran's use of the term also suggests that the teacher is moving away from a detached, self-preoccupied and insensitive detachment to a caring involvement with the learning group. Again, the move is from a deficient state to a more authentic one. This is at odds with the biblical

---

11 This submerged implication, which is present when the imagery of 'incarnation' is used (as it commonly is – see e.g. Harris, 1987:8-9) to describe a full-bodied living out of the truth, as opposed to abstract intellectual affirmation, is the reason for our hesitation over the lan-guage of 'incarnation' in chapter 3.

picture of a God already deeply attuned to his people's suffering, reaching out in mercy to walk among them. It also runs deeply counter to the biblical idea that human nature had nothing to recommend it as a vehicle for redemption (Christ made himself "nothing", "a slave"), suggesting instead that our flesh somehow made God more authentic. Humility is in danger of inverting into pride.

Now our interest here is not primarily in the details of Curran's educational theory, but rather in how we can judge his use of biblical imagery to be faithful or unfaithful to the Bible.[12] The attempt made here at evaluating some of Curran's ideas does involve assessing the beliefs implicit in his metaphors and comparing them with a biblical worldview. But since his metaphors are drawn directly from the Bible, it also involves attempting to discern whether they function to faithfully evoke the contours of the biblical context from which they were drawn. This is the reverse side of what we described earlier. If successful, a metaphor drawn from Scripture can evoke scriptural themes and stories, drawing the thought-world of the Bible into the heart of educational reflection. If unsuccessful, then tensions emerge between the imagery as used in the biblical context and the sense of things evoked by its new educational use. Metaphors can draw the Bible into interaction with education in ways which provoke a wide range of fresh perceptions, but this does not mean that there are no limits, that anything goes, or that we do not need to proceed with considerable care.

Metaphor and intimacy

The interpretation of systematically employed metaphors is, then, to a significant degree contextually bound, and it is possible to make judgements concerning the faithfulness of an educational metaphor to the biblical context. At the same time, the subjective nature of our response to metaphor should not be regarded only as a potential weakness or danger. It can also be a significant strength.

A number of students of metaphor have pointed out that successful metaphors draw us into the world which they evoke. The passage cited in chapter 9, in which John Wilson sought to separate coldly objective prose language from what he saw as a more dangerous poetic

---

12   For a more detailed discussion of Curran's theory, see Smith, 1997b.

language that also engages our imaginations and emotions, shows a clear awareness of this process even as it resists it. Metaphors, like stories, can speak to more parts of our being than our reasoning powers. Ted Cohen argues that metaphors function to establish a peculiar kind of intimacy between speaker and hearer.[13] When an interesting metaphor is used, the hearer must penetrate beyond the surface meaning of the words and work at gaining a sense of the image being conveyed and what it implies, what perceptions it is meant to invoke. The metaphor is a kind of invitation. It does not wear its meaning on its sleeve, and so it invites the hearer to begin to explore its possible meanings, to try it on as a lens for viewing the matter under discussion. It also invites the hearer to bring his or her personal experience into play in order to gain a sense of what the metaphor is getting at. The hearer is drawn into a kind of collaboration with the speaker for communication to take place.

Cohen is well aware that this intimacy does not necessarily imply friendliness. The image could, for instance, be used in order to make a cruel joke at the hearer's expense. If the metaphor is successful, the hearer will nevertheless still have been drawn into the speaker's way of seeing. As Wayne Booth puts it:

> The speaker has performed a task by yoking what the hearer had not yoked before, and the hearer simply cannot resist joining him; they thus perform an identical dance step, and the metaphor accomplished at least part of its work even if the hearer then draws back and says 'I shouldn't have allowed that!'

As we respond to a fertile metaphor we find that our imagination, our experience and our emotions have been engaged, we have been induced to make certain connections between our experiences and to see the world in a certain way. The effects of such seeing can be harder to throw off than an argument offered to us purely in terms of propositions for our intellectual consideration. If we adopt this way of seeing things, making it our own, it can work its way into the ways in which we shape the world around us, affecting our hopes, fears, plans and actions.

---

13   Cohen, 1979.

All of this suggests that the subjective appeal of metaphors can be part of their strength – it is not hard to see here part of the reason why Psalm 23 might hold a less intimate place in the life of the church if it had begun with a propositional statement about God's providence instead of with the line "The Lord is my shepherd". Our response to the metaphoricity of Scripture can, if we dwell upon its metaphors and allow ourselves to be drawn into their world, forge an intimate connection between our lives (not merely our intellects) and the Bible.

It is interesting to note that this addresses what some have come to see as a weakness of linking the Bible to education through worldview statements. In chapter 8 we noted Harry Fernhout's argument that a more propositional approach can be overly cognitive in emphasis. What Christian education should be concerned with, he argues, is a whole life orientation, and not merely a particular way of *thinking* about the world. Thinking Christianly may be essential, but we are eminently capable of thinking one thing and living another. Perhaps metaphor can help to draw further dimensions of our selves (and the selves of our learners) into the process of interacting with Scripture.

This point should not be pressed too far. The process of transforming the way we see and act is not inevitable. Some metaphors remain little more than striking, one-off images, interesting for a moment but soon submerged in the flow of experience. The most original metaphors have a remarkable capacity for being transformed from dramatic overture to clichéd ditty or barely perceived elevator music in a short space of time. Even if we find a metaphor more fertile and begin to explore its broader potential for shaping our seeing, it is only as it becomes systematically embedded in our ways of seeing and living that it will become a "metaphor we live by".[14] Coming up with an interesting new image will avail little if it is not accompanied by changed patterns of practice. Exploring the possibilities of biblical metaphor will thus make demands on our living, and not just our imagination, returning us to the concerns of chapter 3.

With these qualifications, however, enough has been said here to suggest how metaphor can play a constructive role in drawing educational reflection into interaction with the Bible. This continues to move us beyond the scope of the objections surveyed in chapter 2, which by and large assumed that relationships between propositions

---

14   Lakoff & Johnson, 1980:54-55.

or principles and educational practice were the only kinds of relationship in view. It is a key function of metaphor to enable learning by connecting what would otherwise remain disparate parts of our experience; it is this that makes metaphor a significant strand in the relationship between the Bible and education.

12

The imitation of Christ

An itinerant Jewish teacher was approached by some of his followers who put to him the question "Who is the greatest in the kingdom of heaven?" The teacher did not answer immediately. Instead he looked around and, seeing a little child, he called him. Did he do so by name? We know not, but in some way he made it clear that he wanted this child to come and stand among the adults. The child obeyed because the teacher spoke and acted with a certain authority. The teacher then said to those around him, "I tell you truly that you will never as much as enter the heavenly kingdom unless you change and become like a child. The greatest in this kingdom is the one who has humbled himself to the level of this child." The teacher went on to speak about welcoming children "in his name" and the terrible consequences of causing a child to sin. To be dragged gasping for breath to the depths of the sea by the dead weight of a millstone would be a far better destiny. "Gouge out the eye that causes you to sin", he said, "for it is better that you should enter life with one eye than be thrown into the fires of hell with two." And he then told them a story about a shepherd who left his ninety-nine sheep on the hills to go in search of one that had wandered away and was lost. "Your heavenly Father, like that shepherd," he said to them, "is not willing that any of these children be lost."

The teacher was, of course, Jesus and the story comes from Matthew chapter 18.

In our study of ways of relating the Bible to education, we come now to models for teaching and learning that we find in the Bible. The Bible may not have much to say about twenty-first century textbooks, curricula, or forms of educational organisation. But its pages are full of teachers and learners, and standing out among them, head and shoulders above the rest in his teaching, is the man of whom it was said "No-one ever spoke the way this man does".[1] We start, therefore, with Jesus as the model teacher.

Jesus as model teacher

Much has been said and written about Jesus the teacher, his teaching style and methods,[2] and it is not the purpose of this book to provide an exhaustive analysis of this subject. Our focus is on the strands of the rope that link the Bible and education, and our concern is to point to the rich variety of these strands and the ways in which they intertwine, rather than to provide an exhaustive analysis of any of them. Nevertheless, it is probably helpful to outline some of the main points that can be made about Jesus as teacher before going on to say something about what this could mean for our thinking about education today.

The Gospels present Jesus as one whose main activities in his three-year ministry were teaching and healing, and there are rather more references to his teaching than to the healings he performed. Teaching language is used in relation to him more often than

---

1   John 7:46.
2   See, for example, Manson, 1935, Kidner, 1984, Perkins, 1990, and especially the intriguingly titled and very rewarding-to-read chapter 6, 'Why didn't Jesus tell Bible Stories?', of Melchert, 1998.

preaching or prophecy language.[3] He was addressed frequently as 'teacher' and the other most common titles given to him in the Gospels were 'lord/master' and 'rabbi', both of which can have pedagogical connotations.

Charles Melchert, in presenting Jesus as a sage-teacher, a teacher of wisdom, lists among the many forms of wisdom saying attributed to Jesus by the Gospel writers: "folk and literary proverbs; antithetical, synthetic, and comparative proverbs; better sayings; numerical sayings; riddles; rhetorical and impossible questions; beatitudes; admonitions and instructions; disputations; and aphorisms".[4] And then, of course, there were also his parables, the feature of his teaching that springs to mind most readily for most of us.

His proverbs and aphorisms sound like the sayings of the Old Testament book of Proverbs: "The eye is the lamp of the body"; "Which of you, if his son asks for bread, will give him a stone?"; "People do not pick figs from thorn-bushes, or grapes from briars".[5] They make use of vivid images from the everyday world of plants and animals and of everyday concrete observations.[6] But, as Melchert points out,[7] they also go beyond conventional wisdom and even challenge and subvert it, e.g. "Love your enemies, do good to those who hate you" and "You have heard … 'Eye for eye …' But I tell you, Do not resist an evil person."[8] His parables too make much use of everyday life events but invite a fundamental reorientation on the part of their hearers. They are, like metaphors, forms of 'seeing as',[9] and invite us to see things differently, in a new light. As the short narratives they are, they beckon and hint towards a change of perspective and lifestyle.

---

3   Melchert, 1998:214-215.

4   Melchert, 1998:241.

5   Matthew 6:22; 7:9; Luke 6:44.

6   These images were themselves often rooted in the Hebrew scriptures rather than simply chosen by Jesus from among things in the everyday world of his time, e.g. the links between the parable of the mustard seed and the cedar shoot in Ezekiel chapter 17 or the tree of Nebuchadnezzar's dream in Daniel chapter 4.

7   Melchert, 1998:242-245.

8   Luke 6:27; Matthew 5:38-39.

9   Melchert, 1998:248.

Jesus often leaves things deliberately open. His sayings, stories and, not least, his constant use of questions all seem designed to "tease into active thought"[10] rather than provide all the answers, to jolt out of the taken-for-granted and set us off on a new path. They can have multiple interpretations according to our situations and needs. Walter Wink says, "Parables have hooks all over them; they can grab each of us in a different way, according to our need."[11] Those who have ears to hear, let them hear.

This effect is heightened by the "wit and zest" with which he put things. Derek Kidner writes:

> Think of that engaging rogue, the unjust steward, managing not only to outsmart his employer but to get the man's customers and tenants nicely compromised as well (and unable to say 'No' whenever he might turn up for a little hospitality later on). Or that battleaxe of a widow who reduces Judge Jefferies' ancestor to a jelly. Or again those wild exaggerations (too familiar to us now) like the man who has a camel in his cup but only notices the fly; or the idiot who would tempt pigs with a pearl necklace. And then there is that teasing mockery about the prophets who are so conveniently dead. 'You're the old firm, aren't you! Your fathers did the killing, you put up the monuments.'[12]

But the training that Jesus gave his followers involved rather more than their sitting at his feet and listening to what he said. They were trained more as 'apprentices' than as students:

> Discipleship as Jesus conceived it was not a theoretical discipline ... but a practical task to which men were called to give themselves and all their energies. Their work was not to study but to practise. Fishermen were to become fishers of men, peasants were to be labourers in God's vineyard or God's harvest-field. And Jesus was

---

10   From C. H. Dodd's definition of parable quoted in Melchert, 1998:246.
11   Wink, 1989:161 quoted in Melchert, 1998:257.
12   Kidner, 1984:11.

their Master, not so much as a teacher of right doctrine, but rather as the master-craftsman whom they were to follow and imitate.[13]

The model teacher was himself the model of that which he taught. He embodied the character that he set forth as the ideal. This is seen as clearly as anywhere else in the account of his washing of his disciples' feet. After he had done it, he said to them, "You call me 'Teacher' and 'Lord', and rightly so, for that is what I am. Now that I, your Lord and Teacher, have washed your feet, you also should wash one another's feet."[14]

All in all, this is a very inviting picture. Here we have a model for our teaching, one in whose teaching style there is so much to attract and from whom it would seem we can have much to learn for our teaching in our day. But that was then and there and we are in the now and here. Is there not a huge gap between cultures, times and situations which makes it difficult to see exactly how this model can work for us in twenty-first century classrooms? Is there not a cultural objection to reading off from what Jesus said and did what we should say and do with our students?[15]

The cultural objection

We saw earlier some of the objections to linking the Bible with education that were expressed by Paul Hirst and others. One of these was to the effect that in practice efforts to abstract educational principles from what the Bible has to say and then to apply them to schools in our day do not yield anything of substance. Hirst claims that to "take ideas of social control out of a biblical, social context, and transfer them directly

---

13 Manson, 1935:237-270 quoted in Giles, 1981:8.

14 John 13:13-14.

15 Indeed, it could also be objected that there is a gap between the subject-matter of Jesus' teaching and that of the twenty-first century teacher of, say, mathematics or physics as opposed to, say, theology. We would suggest, however, that our openness to be shaped by the influence of Jesus the teacher operates at a deeper level, concerned with those things that are generic to the activity of teaching, e.g. its relational aspect.

to an East End school in our twentieth-century industrial society is patently ludicrous".[16] The indirect route of abstraction and application, however, leads to disagreement on both biblical interpretation and particular applications. Hirst's example concerned taking ideas about discipline and punishment from the Bible, but could not a similar thing be said of any effort we might make to use Jesus as a model for our teaching? Does it require a sandal-clad itinerant lifestyle? No? So we cannot directly imitate what he did; are we not therefore into the same inconclusive process of abstraction and application?

However, a closer look at this objection reveals that it makes much of the need for agreement. It seems to require detailed prescription in order to have anything of any substance. This suggests a very mechanical view of teaching whereby all good teachers teach in identical ways to one another and all right-minded teachers think alike. Is such detailed agreement what we should seek? It is surely in the nature of personhood that we will have our personal styles and approaches in all their rich diversity. Taking Jesus as the model or paradigm teacher does not require us either to copy in slavish detail what we see in him or to abstract principles and apply them in some exact way to our teaching. The imitation of Christ is more about acting in the spirit of what he did than about either literal copying of everything he did or a rational process of abstracting principles and applying them. We may not literally wash our students' feet (perhaps in some circumstances we should consider the possibility of doing so!) but this hardly means that we should not be characterised by a servant-attitude. How precisely this might work out in a particular situation may not be something that we can prescribe in advance, but it does not follow that it cannot make a real difference in practice. And in many present-day educational contexts this would be as radical as it apparently was for Jesus in his day.

This is a matter of being shaped by exposure to the example of Jesus (an example which integrates precept, story, image and action) through immersion in the gospel accounts and the transforming work of the Holy Spirit. Taking the teaching of Jesus as a model for our teaching of our students is therefore not simply a matter of abstracting principles from the Gospel accounts of his teaching and applying them. It is not here a cognitive matter of inferring a way of proceeding and deciding to implement it. Insofar as it is, this comes under the

---

16   Hirst, 1971:306.

heading of the beliefs-to-practices model of chapters 4 and 5. Opening oneself to the influence of a person's actions is both more open-ended and more widely pervasive than, say, using a manual to take apart the engine of a car. And openness is an important ingredient in this. The danger is that we read back into the example of Jesus what we already take for granted as good teaching. The challenge is to open ourselves and our practices and prejudices to the possibility of seeing them all differently. Here again N. T. Wright's analogy of the performing of the missing Act V of a Shakespearean play that we have referred to in chapter 5 becomes relevant. There is ever a need of a movement to and fro between the act being prepared and the four acts already given, between the practices we engage in and the model provided for us in the Gospel accounts of Jesus. The process requires humility, openness to change and imagination to see new possibilities. It is more like painting a picture in the style of the master than following the instructions in a technical manual, more a matter of teaching as an art than teaching as a technique.

Knowledge is seen here in personal terms. It is not knowing *that* something is the case, although it will include elements of this, but more a matter of knowing in a relational sense, knowing another person and, in knowing them, knowing how and when to say or do things in relation to them.[17] It is a matter of coming to know a person through the Bible, a living person whom we meet in the pages of scripture and who is actually present in our situation. It is in seeing him, contemplating him that we are "being transformed into his likeness with ever-increasing glory" and, as this passage makes clear, this is the work of the Holy Spirit.[18] This is, of course, not to say that all the hermeneutical problems of reading Scripture are sidestepped, but simply that there is an added ingredient in the whole situation which is of enormous significance.

It is important to note that what the Bible calls us to is not to be different but to be faithful.[19] It is often assumed – both by its proponents and its attackers – that for education to be Christian is always and everywhere to be distinctively so. Following this line, we may look at how Jesus taught his followers and conclude that there is much there

---

17 Cf. Blomberg, 1998.

18 2 Corinthians 3:18.

19 Cf. Wolterstorff, 1989.

that is generally acknowledged as good teaching practice anyway. But the call to faithfulness does not demand differences at every point. And anyway, it is arguable that what is affirmed as good teaching practice in the example of Jesus may actually be seen as good practice on a wider basis because our culture with its educational practices is already deeply influenced by the example of Jesus, the teacher.

We have focused thus far on the model provided by Jesus as teacher. There are, of course, other ways in which Jesus is a model to us in matters relevant to education. For example, he provides a model of knowing and knowing is a central matter in education. Paul Moser puts it as follows:

> Spiritual communion with God as Father requires filial knowing of God, involving trust, love, prayer and obedience towards God as Father. Such filial knowing finds its unique paradigm in Jesus, the Father's unique Son. ... In restoring the central views of Jesus on knowing God to their place of first importance, we shall open ourselves to the kind of liberating power characteristic of the life and ministry of Jesus.[20]

Moser goes on to explore the implications of taking Jesus the knower as a model for our knowing, and thus provides another example of Jesus as an educational model.

'If a child should ask …'

Jesus stands out as a teacher and is generally acknowledged as such. But the Gospel accounts of the teaching of Jesus are not the only place in the Bible where we may find models for our educational practices. We turn now to the Old Testament *Torah* (Genesis-Deuteronomy) and, in particular, to a passage that is often taken as a starting point in discussions of education and Christian belief: Deuteronomy chapter 6. The chapter comes immediately after a brief account of the Ten Commandments and how they were given by God and before a whole series of chapters containing detailed decrees and laws telling the

---

20   Moser, 1999:601.

people how they should live. Moses is recorded as urging the people to love the Lord their God with all their heart, soul and strength, and to impress the commandments upon their children. He says,

> Talk about them when you sit at home and when you walk along the road, when you lie down and when you get up. Tie them as symbols on your hands and bind them on your foreheads. Write them on the doorframes of your houses and on your gates. (Verses 7-9)

After further urging to obedience, Moses says,

> In the future, when your son asks you, "What is the meaning of the stipulations, decrees and laws the Lord our God has commanded you?" tell him: "We were slaves in Egypt, but the Lord brought us out of Egypt with a mighty hand. Before our eyes the Lord sent miraculous signs and wonders – great and terrible – upon Egypt and Pharaoh and his whole household. But he brought us out from there to bring us in and give us the land that he promised on oath to our forefathers. The Lord commanded us to obey all these decrees and to fear the Lord our God, so that we might always prosper and be kept alive, as is the case today. And if we are careful to obey all this law before the Lord our God, as he commanded us, that will be our righteousness. (Verses 20-25)

In his exploratory study of canon as a model for biblical education,[21] Walter Brueggemann argues that this exchange between

---

21   Brueggemann, 1982. Brueggemann's work has its roots in the theological reaction to the historical critical movements, which sought to get behind the text of scripture to something more authoritative and reliable. This reaction was led by Brevald Childs and James Sanders and it took the canon of scripture as a given and focused on its shape, e.g. the order of its books, and on the processes by which it becomes normative. Important works here are Childs, 1970, 1985; Sanders, 1972, 1984, 1987. See also an account strongly influenced by Brueggemann's work and focused on higher education in Spina, 1989.

child and parent or between learner and teacher (along with other similar exchanges recorded in Exodus and Joshua[22]) provide us with a paradigm of a mode of teaching and learning.[23] To be sure, as we shall see in the next chapter, this is but one of several modes, all of which are important to a whole education process but, for the moment we will focus on this one. It begins in "the yearning of the child to belong to the secret" known by the adults in the community. The child asks about the *meaning* of the decrees and laws (or, in Exodus, of the passover meal or, in Joshua, of the twelve stones set up beside the river Jordan) but the response does not provide a direct explanation. There is what Brueggemann terms "important slippage"[24] between the child's question and the adult's response. The child has asked for an explanation but the adult says, "Let me tell you a story", and that's it – no exhaustive logical explanation nor any 'moral' that is separate from the story and of which the story is merely a vehicle. The story is, as Brueggemann puts it, "the bottom line ... told and left, and not hedged about by other evidences ... not like a preacher who adds two paragraphs after the manuscript, as if to buttress and reinforce it".[25] He writes,

> The Torah does not answer every question. It picks the ground quite selectively. The response of the adult is authoritative. It does not let the child determine the ground. But it is also honest to the child. It concedes ignorance. More than that, it honors mystery. It assures the child that there is much that we do not know and cannot know.[26]

The narrative is *presented*, it is a gift to the child. It sets out an orderly, trustworthy life-world wherein the child can feel safe. Brueggemann suggests we divest the idea of 'Torah' of the narrow and forbidding connotations of 'law', and see it instead, in a way that is more true to its nature, "as an articulation of world

---

22   Exodus 12:26; 13:8; 13:14; Joshua 4:6; 4:21.
23   Brueggemann, 1982:14-39.
24   Brueggemann, 1982:21.
25   Brueggemann, 1982:26.
26   Brueggemann, 1982:22.

coherence, as a shaping of reliable order, as a barrier against the chaos that waits so close".[27]

It is important to repeat that Brueggemann does not present Torah education as the whole of biblical education. There are other modes modeled in the Old Testament canon. But, at the same time, this particular mode is not one that we leave behind in early childhood, with other modes reserved until later. All persons "face the threat of darkness … grow weary of dispute and questioning and risk … need those times of 'homecoming' when they can return to the sureties which do not need to be defended or doubted". Torah is, he says, "finally intergenerational" – it is not only for the young but for all generations.[28]

… and in our day?

This example of a biblical model for teaching is quite different from that of Jesus as the model teacher. The narrative element is present in both but the focus here is not on an individual teacher with his disciples but on a community educating the next generation and giving to it an orderly life-world. We focused on Jesus as turning certainties upside down for his listeners (although, as we shall see in the next chapter, there are other modes of teaching also present in the Gospel accounts), whereas here the certainties are passed on. Even then, it is important to note that these certainties are not universally accepted;

---

27 Brueggemann, 1982:19, referring to the strange darkness of chaotic waters depicted in Jeremiah 5:22. This nomos is given so we are neither without nomos (anomic) nor left to construct and validate our own nomos (autonomous).

28 Brueggemann, 1982:21. Hirst would term this a *primitive* conception of education. For him, the Torah would express "the view of education a primitive tribe might have, when it seeks to pass on to the next generation its rituals, its ways of farming and so on, according to its own customs and beliefs". We need instead a "more sophisticated" concept (Hirst, 1971:308). Against this two points must be emphasised. One is that Brueggemann does not present the Torah mode as the only mode, and neither shall we. The other is his point about our needing a "homecoming" at all ages and stages in life. This mode is not primitive in a cultural sense, nor is it primitive in terms of individual development.

indeed they are quite radical alternatives to the life-worlds of the Canaanites and other peoples within and around Israel.

Application of this model to our day, Brueggemann suggests, would lead us towards a fairly conservative, teacher-centred educational model in which sure truths are passed on with authority. The key point in a canonical approach, however, is to look not just at one particular model, but at the constellation of educational models offered by the canon as a whole. The Torah offers us a model of teaching which projects a stable and secure life-world; other parts of the canon offer other models, and it is to these that we will turn in the next chapter.

13

Further biblical models

The time is the eighth century before Christ. A shepherd leaves a small village which lies a few miles south of Bethlehem in the hills of Judah. He is setting out to travel to Bethel, the chief city in the northern kingdom of Israel. Somebody else must keep his sheep and tend his fig trees because, for now, he has more important and more urgent work to do. The shepherd is a man with a message for kings and peoples, especially for the king and people of Israel. "The lion has roared", he shouts, "Who will not fear?" He speaks not of a mighty beast that he has heard in the thicket, where it prowled seeking animal or even human prey. This lion is the Sovereign Lord, Israel's and Judah's God, and the shepherd who tells of his presence is the one we know as Amos the prophet. "The Sovereign Lord has spoken," he calls out again, "Who can but prophesy?"

The Lion-King, the Lord "roars from Zion and thunders from Jerusalem". What does he say? This is what the Lord says, through

Amos his prophet. There is a judgment coming, and it is coming for all of Israel's neighbours, for Phoenicia and Aram to the north, Ammon to the east and Philistia, Edom and Moab to the south. None is spared, not even the southern kingdom of Judah, for the Lord will send fire upon it that will eat up even the fortress-city of Jerusalem.

Up to this point, there are probably eighth century BC equivalents of 'Amen!' and 'Preach it, brother!' from the audience. However, all of this is but the prologue to the main message of the shepherd-prophet. This message is for Israel, for the people among whom Amos now stands and for Jeroboam their king. For them the roar is loudest and longest. The lion neither roars in the thicket nor growls in his den when he has caught no prey. They will not escape what is to come, neither the swift nor the strong, neither the warrior nor the horseman. The fact that the Lord has chosen them and brought them out of Egypt and into this land of milk and honey will not save them. Their sacrifices, tithes and offerings will not help them. For they have trampled on the poor, oppressed the righteous and "turn(ed) justice into bitterness". Will any be saved? This is what the Lord says: "As the shepherd saves from the lion's mouth only two leg bones or a piece of an ear, so will the Israelites be saved". Not even two legs of lamb, just their bones! But these words speak of hope on the far side of the darkness, of a new day that is coming. The Lord will then restore the ruins of Israel, he will plant his people in their own land, never again to be uprooted. On that day, says the Lord their God through Amos the prophet, "new wine will drip from the mountains and flow from all the hills".[1]

Amos is a true prophet. His recorded speeches display all the marks of prophetic literature: their account of both his own call and credentials and those of Israel, his pleas to the people to repent and to God to relent, the pronouncements of judgements and the promises of restoration.[2]

What, you ask, can all this have to do with education and schooling in the twenty-first century? The disruptive ministry of the prophet seems far removed from the activity of today's teachers! What relevance can this have to classroom education nearly three millennia

---

1   The quoted phrases are from Amos 3:8, 1:2, 5:7, 3:12, 9:13.

2   Sanders describes seven different kinds of statement which are characteristic of prophetic literature, all of which are found in the book of Amos – see Sanders, 1972:74-75.

into the future? Much in every way, is the answer that Walter Brueggemann gives us in his book *The Creative Word*.[3]

The prophets and education

We saw in the previous chapter that Brueggemann regards Torah education as a paradigm of a particular mode of teaching and learning. But it is not the only mode that he finds in the Old Testament scriptures, and to teach as if it were could do the community a great disservice. He writes:

> A community which educates its members in the Torah will do them a great service. It will make available a center for life, a core of memory, a focus around which to organise all of experience. But if a community educates only in the Torah, it may also do a disservice to its members. It may nourish them to fixity, to stability that becomes rigidity, to a kind of certitude that believes all of the important questions are settled. The answers need only to be recited again and again.[4]

Can it not be said of much Christian education in churches and probably also in schools and homes that this rings true? Sadly, all too often this is the dominant mode. What else is needed? Brueggemann's first answer is that we also need the prophetic mode of teaching.

But what do Amos and his fellow-prophets have to add to our understanding of learning and teaching? Prophecy and teaching seem a bit far removed from each other. Prophecy is popularly seen to be essentially a matter of foretelling the future. The word has connotations of magical prediction, something not too different from astrological utterances. These specially gifted people can see further than the rest of us and we hang upon their words for the fate of planet earth. But this popular understanding misses the heart of prophecy by a long way. Its heart is to be found in the task of relating faith and history. Sanders describes the prophets as those that took the faith that the God of Israel was the

---

3   Brueggemann, 1982.

4_   Brueggemann, 1982:40.

Lord of history out of the temple or sanctuary and into "the market-place of human affairs where history was in process". History for the prophets meant "not just the future, but past, present and future – the present and immediate future viewed in light of the past".[5] The past is seen through the stories of the Torah, and this provides for continuity between the Torah and the prophets. However, the prophets also critique the community's settled understanding of the Torah and move beyond it. As Brueggemann puts it,

> ... the Torah is the 'Yes' of God to Israel (2 Cor. 1:19).
> Yes, I will be your God. Yes, you are my people. Yes, I
> will be with you. The prophets add a critical footnote to
> all of this. 'Yes, but what if ...' Thus there is a tension
> between Torah and prophets which must always be
> attended to in education. The tension is the dialectic of
> establishing or *asserting the consensus*, and then raising
> questions which break or challenge or *criticize the con-
> sensus* for the sake of a new word from the Lord. The
> two divisions (Torah/prophets) of the canon together
> suggest that education is a nurture of a restlessness with
> every old truth for the sake of a new truth which is just
> breaking upon us.[6]

The poetic imagination of the prophets seeks to provide a different context for life in the world by "creating a different presumptive world which is buoyed by different promises, served by different resources, sobered by different threats and which permits different decisions".[7] The prophets call their hearers to step outside the familiar, to see everything differently, to nurture their flights of thought with new metaphors, to refuse the domesticating pressures of the convention-ally mediocre. The prophets stand for an openness to spiritual reality beyond the bounds of the dominant rationality of the culture. Their claim to speak in God's name challenges the belief of the powerful that decisions all rest in their hands.[8] A mode of teaching oriented to

---

5   Sanders, 1972:55.
6   Brueggemann, 1982:41.
7   Brueggemann, 1982:52.
8   See also Brueggemann, 1978.

the prophets will not simply tell students "this is the way it is", but will seek creative and vivid ways of making them feel that things should be profoundly *different* from the way they are now. It will point to the sinful distortions of life as presently lived and seek to awaken a hunger for change.

In an article on educating for social justice,[9] Clarence Joldersma provides examples which could illustrate such a mode of teaching in action. He questions the wisdom of encouraging the trait of self-sacrifice in a young African-American woman who exhibits a caring gift when the character of that gift is partially a consequence of being female in a marginalised group of people. He asks whether we can wholeheartedly celebrate a would-be cheerleader making the squad because of her looks or body shape when we ought to question the value system which defined her success, "a social injustice embedded in the current configuration of cheerleading". He suggests that service learning experiences which purport to help 'urban street kids' may reinforce stereotypes in the minds of the participating students if they themselves are not also helped to see "the more complex nature of the problem, including the students' own implicit role in creating that situation by virtue of being part of a privileged socio-economic or racial group". Joldersma goes on to say,

> Seeking shalom needs a *critical* side, one that engages students to become 'sites of resistance' with a healthy dose of distrust of the status quo injustices in which they are embedded.[10]

So we have a second mode of teaching and learning in the Old Testament canon. We need both. If all is the promotion of stability, security and continuity, we have an education which fixes and fossilises and accepts the world as it is too complacently. If all is the questioning of the received ways of thinking and acting, we have an education which deprives learners of any stable place to stand. However, Brueggemann

---

9   Joldersma, 2001; the article is a response to Stronks & Blomberg, 1993.

10   These examples come from pages 110, 111, 113 and 114 of Joldersma's article. A well-known example of a Christian educator whose work is in this mould is Paulo Freire (Freire, 1996a, 1996b), whose pedagogy seeks to evoke a critical awareness of injustice and promote social change.

goes on to suggest that we have more even than this to learn from the shape and processes of Old Testament literature and he turns his attention to the third major division, that known as the Writings.

Wisdom added to knowledge

The Writings are the third division of the Hebrew Bible. They are in a way the 'everything else' that is left after we have taken the books of the Law and the Prophets. They include the Psalms and the Wisdom literature (Job, Proverbs, Ecclesiastes) and also 1 and 2 Chronicles, Ezra and Nehemiah, Ruth, Esther, Song of Songs, Lamentations and Daniel. They therefore contain: the historiography of the chronicler, the short stories of two women in very contrasting settings, a love song, an elegiac lament at the fall of Jerusalem, the apocalyptic visions of a Jew in Babylon as well as a dramatic poem in which the writer wrestles with the paradox of the suffering of the righteous, the parables, riddles and aphorisms culled from contemporary proverbs, and the philosophical questionings of the searcher for meaning in the face of apparent meaninglessness.

It is in these writings that Brueggemann discerns a third mode of teaching and learning, one that focuses on the discernment of order in everyday living, on the exploration of the potential and limitations of individual and communal experience. The emphasis is on the wisdom that must accompany the knowledge given in the story and critically evaluated under prophetic questioning. This, of course, is not detached spectator knowledge but the 'on the field' knowing of those who know who they are and to which people they belong. Having all that, how then shall we live? Sanders puts it in this way: "… wisdom stresses realism … The word *wisdom* in the Bible sometimes means the craft of living under God so that disruption is held in check and stability is maximised".[11]

Between the two poles of the security of our big story and our openness to probing criticism of all our understandings of it, we need to learn to live wisely in all the varied experiences of life, from the ordinary pastoral setting of the cornfield to all the risks of life in royal court, from the ecstasies of loving intimacy to the depths of anguished

---

11   Sanders, 1972:99.

grief, from the soaring flights of the seer to the profundities of the common-sensical.

Wisdom and knowledge go hand in hand through the pages of scripture. The leaders of Israel had their wise men to advise them. The Christian church has its teachers and prophets to whom we flock to hear their words. Where are the wise? Where the love of wisdom? Wisdom is not spectacular. She does not draw the crowds. She is too realistic, too ordinary and everyday. But she calls aloud in the streets and raises her voice in the public squares, "How long will you simple ones love your simple ways?"[12]

Of this third division of the Hebrew scriptures and associated third mode of education, Brueggemann writes:

> ... we have here neither *disclosure* nor *disruption*, but *discernment*. The educational task, then, is to discern and to teach to discern, to attend to the gifts given in experience, to attend to the world around us. It is to read ourselves and that world in its playfulness, to know that what immediately meets the eye is not all there is. It is to know that as we touch the dailyness of our lives, we are in touch also with something precious beyond us that draws close to the holiness of God. In this way we learn that in our knowing we have not been permitted to know fully, but only in a mirror darkly (1 Cor. 13:12).[13]

Similar thoughts are expressed by Charles Melchert in his very helpful book on biblical wisdom and education as he writes:

> One of the major liabilities of contemporary education is the tendency to become a series of isolated specialities that seem to have little to do with learning to live one's daily life in the real world. Wisdom texts have an in-depth concern for the *whole* human condition. Focusing upon the everyday questions of the ordinary individual and community, wisdom texts can help us attend to and

---

12   Proverbs 1:20, 22. 'Simple' in Proverbs generally denotes one without moral direction and inclined to evil.

13   Brueggemann, 1982:75.

learn from birth, life, death, sex, polite manners, sensu-
ality, doubt, pride, injustice, suffering, and other realities
and joys of everyday life. These texts are both intellectu-
ally honest, as they deal with the puzzles and mysteries of
human life and divine presence, and emotionally passionate, as they express and try to make sense of the
pain, the incoherence, the sadness, the despair, and the
exuberant joy of human existence.[14]

Melchert goes on to point out that wisdom texts assume we can
learn from others, even from those outside our cultural and religious
tradition. Proverbs, Job and Ecclesiastes all seem to borrow or adapt
material from Semitic or Egyptian sources and they weave it into a
framework of Hebrew thinking. In this way, the material from without is valued for the truths it contains and refined for use by the people
of God in their own way of life.

Melchert also says that the wisdom texts teach that we can find
God in nature as "an arena of divine presence", whilst at the same
time being sensitive to the limits of our understanding of Him.
Brueggemann suggests that there is a playfulness and delight in the
discerning of wisdom in experience, not only good humour but also
the 'play' that we find in a steering-wheel, "slippage that cannot be
overcome or explained" for "to want more certainty is to crush the
wonder that belongs to knowing".[15] Melchert writes in similar vein:

Sometimes they tell the reader-learner *what to do*
(which is the teacher-author's task), but more often
they tell the reader *how to steer* (which is the learner's
task). They make observations and invite or tease
readers into drawing their own conclusions, to be prac-
tised and tested in life experience, which learners must
do for themselves.[16]

There is a sense of the interconnectedness of all things but we cannot see in our darkling mirror just how and where many of these

---

14   Melchert, 1998:3.
15   Brueggemann, 1982:80; cf. Johnston, 1987.
16   Melchert, 1998:59.

connections are to be made.[17] A growing ability to make these connections, to discern how to 'steer' through life wisely, is perhaps most clearly and poignantly evident in areas such as learning about human relationships or making career choices. However, the need for wisdom is also present across the wider curriculum, for instance in learning about how to relate to the natural world.

The significance of the canon

Having considered some educational models implicitly present in the Torah, the prophets and the writings, we can now stand back and consider why the concept of canon is so important to Brueggemann's argument, and what makes it a distinct addition to our range of approaches to the Bible and education. Clearly, Brueggemann has been involved in interpreting various particular statements, stories and images in the Hebrew scriptures and exploring their educational implications. However, he goes beyond examining individual passages and invites us to consider the implications of the fact that the Bible, in its final canonical form, contains this *range* of pedagogical emphases standing in this particular relationship to one another.

In other words, it is not enough to note that this or that passage of Scripture models this or that pedagogical emphasis; we should go on to ask what overall collection or pattern of emphases is modelled by the Bible as a whole. As Brueggemann points out, the Torah comes first and provides the foundation, a stable sense of identity, but it comes to need the word of prophet, which both builds upon the Torah and criticises the complacent consensus which it can engender. Within this secure-yet-vulnerable context of Torah and prophets the Writings invite us to explore the meaning of our experience of the world around us. Accepting these different texts as *canonical*, as carrying authority when taken together, seems to imply that not only individual passages but also this overall pattern of pedagogical emphases should be taken seriously.[18]

---

17   On wisdom and pedagogy see further Blomberg, 1998; Blomberg, 1986. See also Groome, 1980:139-151.

18   This point is developed in relation to college education by Spina (1989).

This is an addition to the approaches considered thus far in this book for two reasons. First, it raises the possibility that the results of the various strategies for relating the Bible to education could, even if successful on their own terms, still be unbiblical in terms of the bigger picture. We could immerse ourselves sensitively and creatively in the statements, stories, exhortations and images of the Torah, but the results would still be partial. They would not reflect the other canonical emphases, the critical challenge of the prophets and the exploratory wisdom of the writings. A canonical approach emphasises the need to attend to the whole, and to find in it correctives to our natural propensities as teachers. Am I mostly a Torah teacher, committed to the value of teaching basic truths well? Perhaps I need to hear the warnings of the prophet. Am I more prophetically inclined, eager for my students to question and criticise the deformities of the world around them? Perhaps I need to ask where they will find a secure sense of identity, or what they might gain by watching an ant. Attending to the larger canonical pattern can provide a way of questioning different teaching styles without denying their value.

Second, a canonical approach invites us to attend to a different aspect of the Bible. While the other approaches considered thus far ask us to identify biblical teachings, exhortations, images and stories, a canonical approach invites us to consider the *process and shape* of the biblical canon. We are asked to consider the pedagogical process by which the biblical writings were passed down across the generations, a process recorded in many of the passages discussed above. In other words, what pedagogies were considered right for the communication and preservation of God's truth? We are also asked to consider the overall shape of the final canonical text, its peculiar pattern of emphases and the way it places the pedagogical voices of Torah, prophets and writings in relation to one another.

Back to Jesus

By now the attentive reader may well be feeling a growing gap in the argument: do the Torah, the prophets and the writings by themselves make up the 'overall shape' of the Bible? What of the New Testament? This is indeed a serious point of incompleteness in the way in which a canonical approach to education has been articulated. Brueggemann, whose account is the most extensive, limits himself to the Old Testament, and even there gives little attention to the narrative history books. What about the rest of the Christian canon?

This question immediately returns us to the first biblical model we looked at, that of Jesus the Teacher. In his teaching it is not hard to find exemplified all three modes. Here was someone who, in his mountainside teaching, asserted that he had not come "to abolish the Law and the Prophets". Far from it, he had come to "fulfil" them, to affirm them by filling them out with his life and teaching.[19] The Law truly and rightly said that one should not commit murder or adultery nor divorce one's wife nor break an oath. Here we stand and here he stands. But Jesus the Prophet-Teacher questions our traditional understandings of these commands, understandings that have turned to stone as the centuries have passed. "An eye for an eye" says the Law, but he says "go not one mile but two, go the distance of love, even love of those who would torture you".[20] He refers frequently to Abraham, Moses, David, Solomon, Jonah and thereby roots his listeners in the familiar story of their people but, he asks them, are they truly the children of Abraham, the followers of David's example?

In Jesus we find not only the rooting in the Torah and the prophetic shaking of accepted readings but all this, as we saw in the last chapter, accompanied by the proverbs and riddles, the sayings of wisdom that called again and again for the discerning of experience. Jesus is the 'model of the models' for in his teaching can be seen the three emphases already discussed.

Even having extended Brueggemann's account to include Jesus, there is more work to be done: what is added by the later New Testament books, or by the narrative histories of Samuel, Kings and Chronicles? Nevertheless, enough has been said to enable us to identify the *strategy* at work, one of pointing us to the way in which the Bible, not merely in its several parts but also in its overall shape or pattern, models a particular range of educational emphases. This is the key point for our purposes here. If the existing attempts to work out the implications of this approach remain deficient, that does not

---

19   Matthew 5:17.
20   See Matthew 5:38-42.

necessarily deny the validity of the approach; perhaps there is an invitation here to further work.[21]

And one more thing ...

Early in the process of writing this book, we made a presentation to a conference of Christian educationists in which we outlined the main links we saw between the Bible and education. In the question session after the presentation, one person put her hand up and quietly suggested that we might be missing something from our list. We seemed to be focused on answers, she suggested, perhaps we were missing the way in which the Bible alerts us to new or different questions to be asked in educational discussions.

In his book *The Outrageous Idea of Christian Scholarship*, George Marsden argues that Christianity can shape research agendas for, he says, "Christian motives can determine what fields people go into, what topics they study in those fields, and what questions they ask about those topics".[22] Marsden goes on to instance some examples. These include a study of the French Revolution which broke new ground because it looked at the religious origins of that movement in contrast with the prevailing outlook which sought only secular roots (and naturally only found them). They also include a study of Puritan sermons which was not only focused differently from other Puritan scholarship but also asked a different set of questions: previous scholars had focused on the place of the Puritan mind in American intellectual history; the study discussed by Marsden inquired into Puritan faith as a factor in history, and as a result gave more attention to sources such as the spirituality and devotional practices of the

---

21   The same holds for other weaknesses in Brueggemann's particular account. We find, for instance, his mapping of the three pedagogical emphases of the Old Testament canon onto modern understandings of teacher-centred, critical and child-centred pedagogy loose to the point of being misleading. Nevertheless, even if a simplistic correlation of, say, the Writings with Dewey is inadequate, the broader point about the importance of acknowledging the diverse pedagogical models in Scripture still stands.

22   Marsden, 1997:64.

Puritans.[23] Part of what Christians are called to is living certain questions that their faith leaves them with, and not only to walking in the truths that it supplies.

Here again is this emphasis upon the raising of different questions. And does not the Bible itself provide us with examples of this too? Its 'research agenda' seems to be distinctively focused. When we read the stories of the kings of Israel there seems to be a certain selectivity and even incompleteness about them. The stories are summed up with statements about whether or not the kings did what was right in the eyes of the Lord. But what of the economic progress of the nation under their different rules? What of the gaps in their stories – and the chapters taken up with detail of particular events, e.g. the illness of a foreign army commander, repairs to a temple, the discovery of a dusty old scroll? The lengths of the accounts do not seem proportionate to the lengths of their lives or the relative impacts of their reigns in the world of their time. The accounts we have fit in neither of our categories of biography or history. When we come to them we find that the Bible is pursuing a set of questions which may not be the same as ours, and this underlying set of questions itself offers a model which can redirect our questioning.

The Bible may be linked with education in stimulating questions about neglected aspects or ignored issues. The prevailing view of language teaching, for example, may focus on the cognitive, the affective, the social and, more recently, even the cultural. But what of the spiritual and moral? Are these important not only in religious education and personal and social education where the spiritual and moral are normally seen to be at home? In the teaching of languages? Or mathematics? Or science?[24] The focused agendas of the Bible remind us that we should beware of letting the fashions of the age shape our agendas. Perhaps as important in education as the 'hidden curriculum' (of the underlying worldviews evident in practices and ethos rather than in written statements of mission) is the 'null curriculum', that which is not there at all because the prevailing worldview ignores it or shuts it out.

---

23   Marsden, 1997:65, 71.

24   Such questions about the spiritual and moral dimensions of apparently 'secular' subject areas lay at the basis of the Charis curriculum project. See Shortt, 2000; Smith, 1999.

Education can too easily become the practice of the absence of God or, at least, of some of the central divine concerns that come to the fore in the Bible. With the example of the Bible's different kinds of interests and focuses before us, we may be stimulated to ask questions that would not otherwise be asked. The answers to those questions may not come directly from the Bible nor even easily be found anywhere, but directions are changed and new and better vistas of possibility open up before us.

The modelling function of Scripture, which has been the focus of this chapter and chapter 12, adds to and interpenetrates the approaches discussed earlier in the book. One reason for Christians to take story seriously is because the Bible in general and Jesus in particular seem to honour story as a prime vehicle for learning and understanding. In the same way, the profusion of fertile metaphors in Scripture can lead us to take the role of metaphor in our educational thinking seriously. The Bible's central interest in faith can lead us to place an exploration of the implications of our beliefs high on our agendas, and the imitation of Christ has always been central to the Christian understanding of growth in virtue. Once again we find the various strands of the rope connecting the Bible to education to be intimately intertwined; pursuing any one strand sooner or later brings us into contact with the others. Having considered them all individually, it is time to stand back and see where we have come to.

14

Living the question

We started this book with a question: in what sense could education be 'biblical'? How could the Bible, which does not seem to talk directly about schooling, teaching techniques, or many of the areas of knowledge which have come to form the school and college curriculum, have much to say to present day teaching and learning? How are we to understand Christian claims that the Bible is relevant to educational discussion? An advertisement for a periodical in the UK once had the slogan "I never knew that there was so much in it!" We have attempted to show that this may apply to the Bible as an educational text, that it should in fact be seen as a rich resource for the Christian educator, much richer than we have often taken it to be. The links between the Bible and education are several and varied and the relationships among them are complex and subtle. The possibilities for further exploration stretch out in many directions.

A rope of many strands

Both advocates and opponents of attempts to link the Bible with education have too often worked with too narrow a view of how this might be done. At times the assumption has been that such links must be strictly logical, proceeding either deductively from biblical statements to educational conclusions or inductively by abstracting principles from the Bible and then applying these in educational contexts.

We have argued that the logical strand of the rope linking the Bible with education is much 'thicker' than this. Biblical statements and principles may not only *require* educational conclusions: they may also *disallow* certain beliefs and practices, they may *commend* others and still others they may *permit*. The looser logic of this relationship suggests that the Bible may guide us in our educational practice but in a way that provides for our God-given human creativity to flourish within a bounded range of possibilities. This led us to posit for the Bible a shaping or patterning role in relation to educational designs and practices which makes us focus on whether or not the latter 'fit' or 'comport well' with our whole sets of beliefs rather than on whether they 'follow from' particular beliefs.

This, in turn, suggested further strands to the rope: those of narrative and metaphor. Indwelling the biblical meta-narrative and allowing biblical metaphors to play a formative role in our thought and practice are both ways of linking the Bible to education that cannot be reduced to purely logical links between biblical statements/principles and educational consequences/applications. Both stories and metaphors shape our thought and practice at deep levels and they should not be simply regarded as decorative but unnecessary additions to factual language.

Another strand to the rope is one that itself makes metaphorical use of the biblical idea of incarnation. The Word may 'become flesh' in our lives as Christians in the classroom. It matters what kind of people we are in our relationships with our students. The emphasis is on the personal character of the teacher who is herself or himself the link between the Bible and education. The importance of this emphasis cannot be over-estimated. Without it, all our logical deductions and all our talk of the biblical story or biblical metaphors are mere talk. At the same time, taking seriously an incarnational approach leads quickly to serious reflection on issues of pedagogy and curriculum.

This link between the Bible and education is of great importance but it does not exist on its own.

The question of how we are to 'incarnate' the gospel in our practice as teachers also leads to consideration of the models for teaching that the Bible provides. Standing out from among all these is Jesus himself, the model teacher, who himself exemplifies an integration of other biblical models discerned in the main divisions of the Old Testament canon.

Objections revisited

We noted at the outset the existence of both puzzlement and scepticism regarding claims that education might be 'biblical'. Having surveyed a varied array of examples of what thinking biblically about teaching and learning might involve, we are now in a position to put both the scepticism and the puzzlement in some perspective.

In chapter 2 we discussed three basic objections to the very possibility of relating the Bible meaningfully to present-day education. The first pointed to the cultural and historical gap between ancient Israelite educational practices and the task of teaching in our own context. Much has changed and the curriculum has expanded considerably since biblical times, so how can we be expected to copy what people did back then? The second objection pointed out that the more abstract and general principles which might bridge the gap between Bible times and now do not give us very specific guidance. A whole range of other, more mundane considerations tend to do most of the work in determining our actual actions in the classroom. The third objection argued that the Bible was in any case never intended to address the majority of our current educational concerns – it is a book concerned to speak to us about our ultimate commitments, not about questions concerning child psychology or the technology curriculum.

In the light of the examples discussed in the ensuing chapters, these objections now appear somewhat limited in scope. The first assumes that we will be trying to copy the cultures presented in the Bible mechanically, rather than seeking to share their wisdom. There have indeed been many cultural and educational changes since Bible times. They have not, however, removed the significance for educational thinking of the basic narratives, images, beliefs about the world, or implicit models which subtly guide our notions of teaching and learning in particular directions. There is no less necessity today for a broader vision within which our daily actions make sense. The examples that we have discussed have not been instances of particular pedagogical practices simply being copied or transplanted from ancient Israel into the present-day classroom. Instead they are instances of the worldview of the Bible continuing to resonate in the thinking of believing teachers. Granted that mechanical copying of biblical practices will not get us far, there are still plenty of more supple strands connecting the Bible to educational reflection.

The second objection is limited in at least two ways. First, it lays the emphasis squarely on the idea of biblical *principles*, which in Hirst's case seem to be understood as propositions telling us what ought to be done. We have argued in the foregoing chapters that while this kind of approach does have a role to play, the process of biblical reflection is much broader. In addition to prepositional claims and principles, there is also a significant role for virtues, images, stories and models. This objection, like the previous one, turns out to be concerned with only one strand of a richer, more complex set of connections between scripture and pedagogy.

This objection's other limitation is that it seems to assume that for biblical principles to be doing much of significance they must be able to tell us what to do independently of other considerations. However, none of the approaches explored in this book need commit us to the idea that we simply start with a belief (/image/story/model) and then work our way deductively in a single direction down to educational practices. There is always movement in both directions. Sometimes a particular conviction which we hold will lead us to design things a certain way. Sometimes time spent in the classroom will throw up experiences which cause us to rethink some of our cherished ideas. (How many experienced teachers have all the same beliefs about learners that they had when they started teaching?) Sometimes we may discover a new procedure through happy improvisation and only later work out where it fits in the design and develop beliefs about why it works.

In other words, beliefs do not simply dictate practices, they interact with them and with our growing experience of the world. For example, John Amos Comenius, whose work we discussed in chapter 9, believed that all learners, rich or poor, male or female, were made in God's image. He also held that intellectual gifts were given freely and in varied measure by God and therefore offered no grounds for boasting. As a Christian he also considered humility to be a virtue and pride to be a vice. All of these beliefs contributed to his conviction that education should be for all, that "there is no exception from human education except for non-humans".[1] He went further to claim that there should not be separate schools for rich and poor, male and female, able and weak students. Children of both sexes, children from both wealthy and poor family backgrounds, and children of all levels of intellectual ability should be educated together.

While Comenius' Christian beliefs explicitly guided his educational views here, the relationship is not one-way logical requirement. The coherence of Comenius' views depends, for instance, on the belief that selective schools will tend to foster an unhealthy pride. But this belief could in principle be modified by experience. Suppose that Comenius had in the light of further experience come to believe that pride thrived more in common schools than in selective ones. This discovery would have changed the implications of his Christian beliefs. The perceived implications of our basic beliefs shift as our experience grows. This does indeed make it difficult most of the time to show that a certain practice is *purely* the result of a particular faith commitment, but this does not change the fact that faith is playing a guiding role in our thinking. In place of one-way deduction with guaranteed results we have a more complex interaction between faith and experience.

The third objection, that the Bible is not an encyclopaedia designed to answer all our modern educational questions for us, seems no more devastating than the other two in the light of the varied strands connecting the Bible to education. In fact, none of the examples that we have considered regard the Bible as such an encyclopaedia. Tracing the connections between the Bible and teaching has not forced us to go against the biblical grain, forcing the Bible to be what it is not. Calls to live in the light of redemption, basic claims about issues such as human nature or the meaning of the world, stories and images that invite us to see and live in the world in certain ways, patterns and models offered for imitation across the generations – these are the very stuff of the biblical writings and clearly connect with educational concerns. It is in such connections, and not in the notion that the Bible will offer us a set of prepackaged

---

1   Pampaedia, II:30, in Dobbie, 1986.

answers to our educational questions, that we have sought and found the Bible's relevance to teachers. Agreeing that the Bible is no encyclopaedia does not, then, leave it disconnected from educational concerns.

To those who react to the notion of a 'biblical' approach to teaching with more puzzlement than out and out scepticism, we suggest in the light of the examples surveyed here that the possibilities for developing such an approach are rich and varied. The Bible is connected to education by many strands, any or all of which could and should be explored much more extensively in relation to a host of particular educational contexts and concerns. While a superficial glance at the Bible will yield meagre returns, a deeper wrestling with the claims, challenges, images, stories and patterns of the Bible will yield plenty for believing teachers to chew on.

The Bible as content

This book has not been directly concerned with how the Bible should itself be taught in the classroom, but the issues that we have explored here do have implications for that task. As we noted at the end of chapter 2, simply inserting material drawn from the Bible as educational content does not guarantee that the education offered is in any strong sense 'biblical'. Clearly the Bible has a place in many parts of the curriculum, not only in religious education, but also in areas of study where its influence has been profound, such as history (consider, for instance, the role of biblical faith in the Puritans' migration to America) and literature (consider, for instance, the poetry of a John Donne or George Herbert). Realising the variety of ways in which it can speak can lead us to richer ways of dealing with the Bible as a part of educational content.

As writers, we were involved in a curriculum project a few years ago which produced teacher resource materials for, among other things, the teaching of English literature. The work with which the writing team of teachers of English started was Shakespeare's *Macbeth* and very quickly they found that the materials would be incomplete without a unit of work on the imagery used in the play. A number of the image patterns they found echoed those used in Christian liturgy and the Bible (light and darkness, washing and water, blood, and clothing). Reference to biblical sources, with their distinctive patterns of imagery, can give a fuller understanding of the play and of the times in which it was written and first performed.

At times, some Christian curriculum materials seem to view the Bible largely as a collection of sayings or individual truths to be noted, sung or memorised, or mainly as a collection of stories or doctrines. At times attempts to introduce the Bible across the curriculum are contrived, as when English translations of the Hebrew or Greek of the Bible are used to provide examples of points of English grammar, or the mandate to be fruitful and *multiply* from Genesis is mentioned in an arithmetic lesson about the operations of addition, subtraction, multiplication and division. Such limited attempts should not obscure the possibilities for a deeper encounter with the Bible in various curriculum areas. Studying the different strands connecting the Bible to educational reflection can inform and enrich the ways in which the Bible is handled in the classroom. Approaching the Bible through its claims, exhortations, stories, images and patterns could lead to a more authentic engagement with the text and its fruits than would an approach focused more narrowly on one or two aspects or on the occasional citation of individual sayings taken out of their context.

A core to the rope?

Jesus drew conclusions, often surprising ones, from the statements of the Old Testament scriptures. He went beyond the letter of particular commands and commendations to the spirit of the whole set of scriptural beliefs. He used metaphors freely and told stories frequently. And he lived what he taught and made relationships central to the whole business of living in his father's world. In Jesus the Teacher we see not a list of alternative ways of relating the scriptures to teaching, but rather an embodiment of them all altogether in a way that is far more substantial and attractive than any of these approaches taken individually. In him, to paraphrase Colossians chapter 2 verse 3, are hidden all the treasures of wisdom, knowledge and guidance for Christian education. In his teaching ministry, the strands of our rope do not run side by side, they are woven together.

The various approaches surveyed here belong together, interacting with and supplementing one another. At the outset we compared them to the interwoven strands of a rope. But is any one of the strands more basic or central than the others? Is there a core to the rope or could one of the strands be seen instead as a silver thread through every strand? Some might respond that surely the logical kind of link is the more central for it is the 'tightest' relationship and keeps a check on the others. But others might immediately say to this that without incarnation in lived and loving experience, all else is, in Paul's words, mere sounding brass and tinkling cymbals. Some will urge that our propositional claims and everyday actions only gain sense in the context of a broader story, or that all of our language is in some sense metaphorical, or that the canonical approach offers a framework within which our various propositions, stories and metaphors can be held in balance. We suspect that an argument could be made for any of the strands being taken as the core of the rope, and that our conclusion will depend largely on what we mean by something being 'core' or 'basic' at any given time.

The rope connecting the Bible to education is woven of many strands, and they are deeply intertwined. More linear approaches are complemented and mutually corrected by those which are more a matter of patterning. Propositional claims can place limits on the meaning of metaphors, but also themselves commonly contain and depend upon metaphorical language. Metaphors and stories give rise to, and in turn are made plausible by particular ways of living. Metaphors and statements take on particular meaning within stories. 'Incarnational' approaches and the idea of the Bible modelling educational emphases are close to one another. The idea of teaching as storytelling is a metaphor. The longer one looks, the more interconnections become evident. In practice, the different strands are hard to separate cleanly, and actual examples of Christian educational discussion or practice will tend to draw upon several or all of them, weaving a rounded language of faith from proposition, story, metaphor, model and life lived with God.

It is because of this interweaving of the different strands that we do not think it appropriate to try to present any one of the strands as the most basic or the most important. The different approaches need each other and complete each other. Keeping this in view would help to mitigate the concerns of some who have criticised the common use of the ideas of developing a Christian *mind* or a Christian *worldview* to express how scripture should impinge upon our cultural practices.

Nicholas Wolterstorff, for example, has suggested that focusing on the idea of a Christian worldview

> … puts too much emphasis on a "view", that is, on what we have called cognition. To be identified with the people of God and to share in its work does indeed require that one have a system of belief – call it the Christian world and life view. But it requires more than that. It requires the Christian way of life. Christian education is education aimed at training for the Christian *way of life*, not just education aimed at inculcating the Christian world and life view.[2]

An emphasis on a whole way of life draws in all of the various strands that we have explored. Wolterstorff's reminder that what is ultimately at stake is a Christian way of living, of being and becoming in the community and the world, fits readily with both the modelling strand and the 'incarnation' strand of our rope, but it also draws in the ways in which we see, our hopes, memories and day to day roles, and the beliefs by which we orient ourselves. The different strands gain their vitality as part of a lived whole.

Living the question

This emphasis on Christian living is also relevant to a further objection to the enterprise of thinking biblically about education, one that we discussed in chapter 8. It's all very well describing all these ways in which the Bible could inform education, some will respond, but why would we want it to? For many, any efforts in this direction will appear sinister, either because they believe that the kinds of beliefs and values inspired by the Bible are outdated, wrong or oppressive, or because they fear that these beliefs and values will be imposed in oppressive ways on those who do not share them through the instrument of education.

Note that this is a different kind of objection to the ones considered earlier. In this book we have focused specifically on the question of how the Bible can be meaningfully related to education, and have

---

2   Wolterstorff, 1980:14. See further Fernhout, 1997.

therefore given most of our attention to those objections which claim that it can't be done, that there is no meaningful relationship. The argument that the results will be oppressive is a step further along the path: it accepts that the Bible can lead to particular educational beliefs and practices, but argues that it should not be allowed to do so. We do not wish to reject this concern out of hand. Through the years the Bible has indeed been used to defend ugly prejudices and practices, and it has often been wielded more as a cudgel than as the word of life. Neither can we answer it here at any length. Such an answer would involve defending the Bible and the wider enterprise of Christian education against their critics, a task that lies well beyond the scope of this book.[3] A brief response is nevertheless appropriate, and will sound the note on which we wish to close.

We believe that the darker side of the use of the Bible in different times and places is bound up with human sin. Fallen readers abuse the Bible by turning it to their own ends and using it to shore up their own prejudices and ambitions. As we saw in chapter 8, this process is clearly recognised, described and condemned within the pages of the Bible itself.[4] The best response to it will ultimately be grace-filled counter-examples of repentant and hopeful living in the light of scripture, examples which bear out the Apostle Paul's statement that against such things as love, joy, peace, patience, kindness, goodness, faithfulness, gentleness and self-control there is no law.[5] If these fruits of the Spirit do not animate the results of our efforts to think biblically, we will know that something has gone wrong somewhere along the line. Without the fruits of grace, applications of the Bible will become lifeless or positively harmful.

It is partly for this reason that we have made no attempt in this book to offer a biblical recipe or blueprint for education, instead describing a variety of particular attempts to live as educators in the light of scripture. These attempts are all instances of redemption in progress, episodes along the path of renewal rather than comprehensive solutions to be set in stone. We hope that our attempt to put up some signposts pointing out the broad lay of the land will inspire readers to find other ways of connecting the wisdom of scripture with their

---

3 See further Sandsmark, 2000; Thiessen, 2001.
4 See chapter 8, pages 93-94.
5 Galatians 5:23.

educational tasks, ways which will go beyond what we have outlined. The possibilities for further reflection and research are considerable, both in terms of developing the approaches described here further and in terms of applying them to particular curriculum areas, contexts or educational issues. The question of how the Bible can illuminate the teacher's task is not one to be settled once and for all by laying out a recipe for mechanical adoption; it is a question that must be lived ongoingly by those who have come to recognise in the Bible the words of life.

Bibliography

Adams, J. (1982). *Back to the blackboard*. Phillipsburg, NJ: Presbyterian & Reformed Publishing Co.

Allen, R. T. (1993). Christian thinking about education. *Spectrum, 25*(1), 17-24.

Anthony, E. M. (1963). Approach, method and technique. *English Language Teaching, 17*(2), 63-67.

Badley, K. (1994). The faith/learning integration movement in Christian higher education: Slogan or substance? *Journal of Research on Christian Education, 3*(1), 13-33.

Badley, K. (1996). Two 'cop-outs' in faith-learning integration: Incarnational integration and worldviewish integration. *Spectrum, 28*(2), 105-118.

Baker, D., Dobson, S., Gillingham, H., Heywood, K., Smith, D., & Worth, C. (1998). *Charis Deutsch: Einheiten 6-10*. Nottingham: The Stapleford Centre.

Baker, W. R. (1994). 'Above all else': Contexts of the call for verbal integrity in James 5:12. *Journal for the Study of the New Testament* (54), 57-71.

Bauckham, R. H., Trevor. (1999). *Hope against hope: Christian eschatology in contemporary context.* London: Darton, Longman and Todd.

Beavis, A. K., & Thomas, A. R. (1996). Metaphors as storehouses of expectation: Stabilizing the structures of organizational life in independent schools. *Educational Management and Administration, 24*(1), 93-106.

Black, M. (1993). More about metaphor. In A. Ortony (Ed.), *Metaphor and thought* (2nd ed., pp. 19-41). Cambridge: Cambridge University Press.

Blomberg, D. (1998). The practice of wisdom: Knowing when. *Journal of Education and Christian Belief, 2*(1), 7-26.

Blomberg, D. G. (1986). Wisdom at play: In the world but not of it. In I. Lambert & S. Mitchell (Eds.), *The crumbling walls of certainty: Towards a Christian critique of postmodernity and education* (pp. 120-135). Sydney: CSAC.

Bolt, J. (1993). *The Christian story and the Christian school.* Grand Rapids: Christian Schools International.

Boyd, W. (1956). *Emile for today: The Emile of Jean Jacques Rousseau* (W. Boyd, Trans.). London: Heinemann.

Brueggemann, W. (1978). *The prophetic imagination.* Philadelphia: Fortress Press.

Brueggemann, W. (1982). *The creative word: Canon as a model for biblical education.* Philadelphia: Fortress Press.

Brumfit, C. (1991). Problems in defining instructional methodologies. In K. de Bot & R. P. Ginsberg & C. Kramsch (Eds.), *Foreign language research in cross-cultural perspective* (pp. 133-144). Amsterdam/Philadelphia: John Benjamins.

Bruner, J. (1985). Narrative and paradigmatic modes of thought. In E. Eisner (Ed.), *Learning and teaching the ways of knowing: Eighty-fourth yearbook of the National Society for the Study of Education.* Chicago: National Society for the Study of Education.

Bruner, J. S. (1996). *The culture of education.* Cambridge, Mass.: Harvard University Press.

Burrell, D. B. (1979). Religious belief and rationality. In C. F. Delaney (Ed.), *Rationality and religious belief.* London: University of Notre Dame Press.

Cartwright, B. (1999, January 1). My cheating art. *Times Educational Supplement.*

Carvill, B. (1991a). Foreign language education: A Christian calling. *Christian Educators Journal, 30*(3), 29-30.

Carvill, B. (1991b). Teaching culture from a Christian perspective: Is it any different? *Proceedings Journal of the North American Association of Christian Foreign Language and Literature Faculty, 1*, 13-18.

Childs, B. S. (1970). *Biblical theology in crisis.* Philadelphia: Fortress Press.

Childs, B. S. (1985). *The New Testament as canon: An introduction.* Philadelphia: Fortress Press.

Clines, D. J. A. (1997). *The Bible and the modern world.* Sheffield: Sheffield Academic Press.

Cloete, G. D., & Smit, D. J. (1994). Its name was called Babel. *Journal of Theology for Southern Africa, 86*, 81-87.

Clouser, R. A. (1991). *The myth of religious neutrality: An essay on the hidden role of religious belief in theories.* Notre Dame: Notre Dame University Press.

Cohen, T. (1979). Metaphor and the cultivation of intimacy. In S. Sacks (Ed.), *On metaphor* (pp. 1-10). Chicago: University of Chicago Press.

Cooling, T. (1994). *A Christian vision for state education.* London: SPCK.

Cooling, T. (1996). Education is the point of RE – not religion? Theological reflections on the SCAA model syllabuses. In J. Astley & L. J. Francis (Eds.), *Christian theology and religious education: Connections and contradictions* (pp. 165-183). London: SPCK.

Curran, C. A. (1969). *Religious values in counseling and psychotherapy.* New York: Sheed & Ward.

Curran, C. A. (1972). *Counseling-Learning: A whole-person model for education.* New York: Grune & Stratton.

Curran, C. A. (1976). *Counseling-learning in second languages.* Apple River, IL: Apple River Press.

Davidson, D. (1979). What metaphors mean. In S. Sacks (Ed.), *On metaphor* (pp. 29-46). Chicago: University of Chicago Press.

Davis, A. (1999). Prescribing teaching methods. *Journal of Philosophy of Education, 33*(3), 387-401.

Dobbie, A. M. O. (1986). *Comenius' Pampaedia or universal education.* Dover: Buckland.

Dunne, J. (1993). *Back to the rough ground: Practical judgement and the lure of technique.* Notre Dame: University of Notre Dame Press.

Eco, U. (1999). *Serendipities: Language and lunacy.* London: Phoenix.

Egan, K. (1988). *Teaching as Storytelling.* London: Routledge.

Fackre, G. (1983). Narrative theology: An overview. *Interpretation, 37*, 340-352.

Fackre, G. J. (1984). *The Christian story: a narrative interpretation of basic Christian doctrine* (Rev. ed.). Grand Rapids: W.B. Eerdmans Pub. Co.

Fernhout, H. (1997). Christian schooling: Telling a worldview story. In I. Lambert & S. Mitchell (Eds.), *The crumbling walls of certainty: Towards a Christian critique of postmodernity and education* (pp. 75-98). Sydney: CSAC.

Freire, P. (1996a). Education, liberation and the church. In J. Astley & L. Francis & C. Crowder (Eds.), *Theological perspectives on Christian formation: A reader on theology and Christian education* (pp. 169-186). Leominster: Gracewing.

Freire, P. (1996b). *Pedagogy of the oppressed* (rev. ed.). New York: Continuum.

Giles, K. N. (1981). Teachers and teaching in the church: Part 1. *Journal of Christian Education, 70,* 5-17.

Goldingay. (1994). *Models for scripture.* Carlisle: Paternoster Press.

Griffioen, S. (1998). Perspectives, worldviews, structures. In H. Aay & S. Griffioen (Eds.), *Geography and worldview: A Christian reconnaissance* (pp. 125-143). Lanham: University Press of America.

Grimmitt, M. (1987). *Religious education and human development: The relationship between studying religions and personal, social and moral education.* Great Wakering: McCrimmons.

Grimmitt, M. (1991). The use of religious phenomena in schools: Some theoretical and practical considerations. *British Journal of Religious Education, 13*(2), 77-88.

Groome, T. H. (1980). *Christian religious education: sharing our story and vision.* San Francisco: Harper & Row.

Groome, T. H. (1991). *Sharing faith: a comprehensive approach to religious education and pastoral ministry: the way of shared praxis.* San Francisco: HarperSanFrancisco.

Harris, M. (1987). *Teaching and religious imagination.* San Francisco: Harper & Row.

Hauerwas, S. (1992). On witnessing our story: Christian education in liberal societies. In S. Hauerwas & J. H. Westerhoff (Eds.), *Schooling Christians: "Holy experiments" in American education* (pp. 214-234). Grand Rapids: Eerdmans.

Hauerwas, S., & Jones, L. G. (1989). *Why narrative?: readings in narrative theology.* Grand Rapids: Eerdmans.

Hickam, H. (1998). *Rocket boys: A memoir.* New York: Delacorte Press.

Hill, B. (1976). Teaching as reconciliation. *Journal of Christian Education, Papers 56,* 8-16.

Hill, B. (1978). Is it time we deschooled Christianity? *Journal of Christian Education* (63), 5-21.

Hirst, P. (1971). Christian education: A contradiction in terms? *Faith and Thought*, 99(1), 43-54.

Hirst, P. H. (1974). *Knowledge and the curriculum: A collection of philosophical papers*. London: Routledge & Kegan Paul.

Hirst, P. H. (1976). Religious beliefs and educational principles. *Learning for Living*, 15, 155-157.

Hirst, P. H. (1993). Education, knowledge and practices. In R. Barrow & P. White (Eds.), *Beyond liberal education: Essays in honour of Paul H. Hirst* (pp. 184-199). London: Routledge.

Hopkins, G. M. (1970). That nature is a heraclitean fire and of the comfort of the resurrection. In W. H. Gardner & N. H. MacKenzie (Eds.), *The poems of Gerard Manley Hopkins* (pp. 105-106). Oxford: Oxford University Press.

Howell, R. W., & Bradley, W. J. (Eds.). (2001). *Mathematics in a postmodern age: A Christian perspective*. Grand Rapids/Cambridge: Eerdmans.

Ihde, D. (1993). *Philosophy of technology: An introduction*. New York: Paragon House.

Jandl, E. (1981). *die bearbeitung der mütze*. Darmstadt: Luchterhand.

Johnston, R. K. (1987). Wisdom literature and its contribution to a biblical environmental ethic. In W. Granberg-Michaelson (Ed.), *Tending the garden: Essays on the Gospel and the earth* (pp. 66-82). Grand Rapids: Eerdmans.

Joldersma, C. (2001). Educating for social justice: Revising Stronks' & Blomberg's idea of responsive discipleship. *Journal of Education and Christian Belief*, 5(2), 105-117.

Keatinge, M. W. (1967). *The Great Didactic of John Amos Comenius* (2nd ed.). New York: Russell & Russell.

Keller, J. A. (1989). Accepting the authority of the Bible: Is it rationally justified? *Faith and Philosophy*, 6(4), 378-397.

Kidner, D. (1984). Jesus the Teacher. *Religious Studies Today*, 10(1), 9-12.

Klapwijk, J. (1989). On worldviews and philosophy: A response to Wolters and Olthuis. In P. A. Marshall & S. Griffioen & R. J. Mouw (Eds.), *Stained glass: Worldviews and social science* (pp. 41-55). Lanham: University Press of America.

Klapwijk, J. (1991). Epilogue: The idea of transformational philosophy. In J. Klapwijk & S. Griffioen & G. Groenewoud (Eds.), *Bringing into captivity every thought: Capita selecta in the history of Christian evaluations of non-Christian philosophy*. Lanham: University Press of America.

Kumaravadivelu, B. (1994). The postmethod condition: (E)merging strategies for second/foreign language teaching. *TESOL Quarterly, 28*(1), 27-48.

Kuyper, A. (1931). *Lectures on Calvinism.* Grand Rapids: Eerdmans.

Lakoff, G., & Johnson, M. (1980). *Metaphors we live by.* Chicago/London: University of Chicago Press.

Lakoff, G., & Johnson, M. (1999). *Philosophy in the flesh: The embodied mind and its challenge to Western thought.* New York: Basic Books.

Larsen-Freeman, D. (1991). Research on language teaching methodologies: A review of the past and an agenda for the future. In K. de Bot & R. P. Ginsberg & C. Kramsch (Eds.), *Foreign language research in cross-cultural perspective* (pp. 119-132). Amsterdam/Philadelphia: John Benjamins.

Lee, D. J. (1993). Introduction. In D. J. Lee (Ed.), *Storying ourselves: A narrative perspective on Christians in psychology.* Grand Rapids: Baker Books.

Lundin, R., Walhout, C., & Thiselton, A. C. (1999). *The promise of hermeneutics.* Grand Rapids/Carlisle: Eerdmans/Paternoster Press.

MacIntyre, A. (1971). *Against the self-images of the age: Essays on ideology and philosophy.* London: Gerald Duckworth.

MacIntyre, A. (1984). *After virtue: A study in moral theory* (2nd ed.). London: Duckworth.

Manson, T. W. (1935). *The teaching of Jesus: Studies of its form and content.* Cambridge: Cambridge University Press.

Marsden, G. M. (1997). *The outrageous idea of Christian scholarship.* New York: Oxford University Press.

Marx, L. (1995). The idea of "technology" and postmodern pessimism. In Y. Ezrahi & E. Mendelsohn & H. Segal (Eds.), *Technology, pessimism and postmodernism* (pp. 11-28). Amherst: University of Massachusetts Press.

May, P. (1988). *Confidence in the classroom: realistic encouragement for teachers.* Leicester: IVP.

May, R. (Ed.). (1969). *Existential psychology.* New York: Random House.

Melchert, C. F. (1998). *Wise teaching: Biblical wisdom and educational ministry.* Harrisburg, PA: Trinity Press International.

Mendus, S. (1995). Tolerance and recognition: Education in a multicultural society. *Journal of Philosophy of Education, 29*(2), 191-202.

Middleton, J. R., & Walsh, B. J. (1995). *Truth is stranger than it used to be: Biblical faith in a postmodern world.* Downers Grove, Illinois: IVP.

Moberly, R. W. L. (1986). Story in the Old Testament. *Themelios, 11*(3), 77-82.

Mofeking, T. (1988). Black Christianity, the Bible and liberation. *The Journal of Black Theology, 2,* 34-42.

Moser, P. K. (1999). Jesus on knowledge of God. *Christian Scholar's Review*, 28(4), 586-604.

Moskowitz, G. (1978). *Caring and sharing in the foreign language class: A sourcebook on humanistic techniques*. Cambridge, MA: Newbury House.

Moskowitz, G. (1982). Self-confidence through self-disclosure: The pursuit of meaningful communication. In P. Early (Ed.), *ELT Documents 113 – Humanistic approaches: An empirical view*. London: The British Council.

Munby, H. (1986). Metaphor in the thinking of teachers: An exploratory study. *Journal of Curriculum Studies, 18*(2), 197-209.

Murphy, D. (1995). *Comenius: A critical reassessment of his life and thought*. Dublin: Irish Academic Press.

Neill, S. (1986). *A history of Christian missions*. Harmondsworth: Penguin.

Neufeld, M. J. (1995). *The rocket and the Reich: Peenemünde and the coming of the ballistic missile era*. New York: The Free Press.

Oller, J., & Richard-Amato, P. A. (1983). *Methods that work: A smorgasbord of ideas for language teachers*. Rowley, Mass.: Newbury House.

Olson, B. (1973). *Bruchko*. Chichester: New Wine Press.

Olthuis, J. H. (1979). Towards a certitudinal hermeneutic. In J. Kraay & A. Tol (Eds.), *Hearing and doing*. Toronto: Wedge.

Olthuis, J. H. (1985). On worldviews. *Christian Scholars Review, 14*(2), 153-164.

Olthuis, J. H. (1987). *A hermeneutics of ultimacy: Peril or promise?* Lanham: University Press of America.

Ong, W. J. (1958). *Ramus, method and the decay of dialogue*. Cambridge, Mass.: Harvard University Press.

Ortony, A. (1993). *Metaphor and thought* (2nd ed.). Cambridge: Cambridge University Press.

Palmer, P. J. (1983). *To know as we are known: A spirituality of education*. San Francisco: Harper & Row.

Palmer, P. J. (1998). *The courage to teach: Exploring the inner landscape of a teacher's life*. San Francisco: Jossey Bass.

Pazmiño, R. W. (1997). *Foundational issues in Christian education: An introduction in evangelical perspective*. Grand Rapids: Baker.

Peirce, B. N. (1995). Social identity, investment and language learning. *TESOL Quarterly, 29*(1), 9-31.

Perkins, P. (1990). *Jesus as teacher*. New York: Cambridge University Press.

Plantinga, A. (1982). On Reformed epistemology. *Reformed Journal, 32*, 13-17.

Plantinga, A. (1990). *The twin pillars of Christian scholarship*. Grand Rapids: Calvin College and Seminary.

Plantinga, A. (1996). Methodological naturalism? In J. M. van der Meer (Ed.), *Facets of faith and science* (Vol. 1: Historiography and modes of interaction, pp. 177-221). Lanham: University Press of America/The Pascal Centre for Advanced Studies in Faith and Science.

Plantinga, A. (1998). Advice to Christian philosophers. In J. F. Sennett (Ed.), *The analytic theist: An Alvin Plantinga reader* (pp. 296-315). Grand Rapids/Cambridge: Eerdmans.

Plato, & Waterfield, R. (1994). *Republic*. Oxford/New York: Oxford University Press.

Postman, N. (1996). *The end of education*. New York: Vintage Books.

Prabhu, N. S. (1990). There is no best method – Why? *TESOL Quarterly*, 24(2), 161-176.

Quine, W. V., & Ullian, J. S. (1970). *The web of belief*. New York: Random House.

Quine, W. V. O. (1963). *From a logical point of view: Logico-philosophical papers*. New York: Harper & Row.

Richards, J. C., & Rodgers, T. S. (1982). Method: Approach, design and procedure. *TESOL Quarterly*, 16(2), 153-168.

Richards, J. C., & Rodgers, T. S. (1986). *Approaches and methods in language teaching: A description and analysis*. Cambridge: Cambridge University Press.

Ricœur, P. (1981). *The rule of metaphor: Multi-disciplinary studies of the creation of meaning in language*. Toronto/Buffalo: University of Toronto Press.

Roques, M. (1989). *Curriculum unmasked: Towards a Christian understanding of education*. Sutherland: Albatross.

Ryken, L. (1979). *Triumphs of the imagination: Literature in Christian perspective*. Downers Grove: IVP.

Sacks, S. (Ed.). (1979). *On metaphor*. Chicago: University of Chicago Press.

Sanders, J. A. (1972). *Torah and canon*. Philadelphia: Fortress Press.

Sanders, J. A. (1984). *Canon and community: A guide to canonical criticism*. Philadelphia: Fortress Press.

Sanders, J. A. (1987). *From sacred story to sacred text*. Philadelphia: Fortress Press.

Sandsmark, S. (2000). *Is world view neutral education possible and desirable? A Christian response to liberal arguments*. Carlisle/Nottingham: Paternoster Press/The Stapleford Centre.

Sartre, J.-P. (1957). *Existentialism and human emotions*. New York: Philosophical Library.

Schaller, K. (1992). Erziehung zur Menschlichkeit, Komenskys kritischer Beitrag zu Gegenwartsproblemen der Erziehung. In K. Goßmann & C. T. Scheilke (Eds.), *Jan Amos Comenius 1592-1992: Theologische und pädagogische Deutungen* (pp. 17-30). Gütersloh: Gerd Mohn.

Schön, D. A. (1993). Generative metaphor: A perspective on problem-setting in social policy. In A. Ortony (Ed.), *Metaphor and thought* (2nd ed., pp. 137-163): Cambridge University Press.

Schwehn, M. (1993). *Exiles from Eden: Religion and the academic vocation in America*. New York: Oxford University Press.

Segal, H. P. (1995). The cultural contraditions of high tech: Or the many ironies of contemporary technological optimism. In Y. Ezrahi & E. Mendelsohn & H. Segal (Eds.), *Technology, pessimism and postmodernism* (pp. 175-216). Amherst: University of Massachusetts Press.

Shakespeare, W. *Hamlet*.

Shortt, J. (1991). *Towards a Reformed epistemology and its educational significance*. Unpublished PhD, University of London, London.

Shortt, J. (2000). The rationale of the Charis project. In M. Leicester & C. Modgil & S. Modgil (Eds.), *Spiritual and religious education* (pp. 160-170). London: Falmer Press.

Shortt, J., Smith, D., & Cooling, T. (2000). Metaphor, Scripture and education. *Journal of Christian Education, 43*(1), 22-28.

Simon, H. A. (1990). A mechanism for social selection and successful altruism. *Science, 250*, 1665-1668.

Smith, D. (1995). Christian thinking in education reconsidered. *Spectrum, 25*(1), 9-24.

Smith, D. (1997a). Communication and integrity: Moral development and modern languages. *Language Learning Journal, 15*, 31-38.

Smith, D. (1997b). In search of the whole person: Critical reflections on Counseling-Learning. *Journal of Research on Christian Education, 6*(2), 159-181.

Smith, D. (1999). Cross-curricular spiritual and moral development: Reflections on the Charis Project. *Journal of Christian Education, 42*(2), 27-34.

Smith, D. (2000a). Faith and method in foreign language pedagogy. *Journal of Christianity and Foreign Languages, 1*(1), 7-25.

Smith, D. (2000b). Gates unlocked and gardens of delight: Comenius on piety, persons and language learning. *Christian Scholar's Review, 30*(2), 207-232.

Smith, D. (2000c). Spirituality and teaching methods: Uneasy bedfellows? In R. Best (Ed.), *Educating for spiritual, moral, social and cultural development* (pp. 52-67). London: Cassell.

Smith, D. I., & Carvill, B. (2000). *The gift of the stranger: Faith, hospitality and foreign language learning.* Grand Rapids: Eerdmans.

Soskice, J. M. (1985). *Metaphor and religious language.* Cambridge: Cambridge University Press.

Spina, F. A. (1989). Revelation, reformation, re-creation: Canon and the theological foundation of the Christian university. *Christian Scholar's Review, 18*(4), 315-332.

Staudenmaier, J. M. (1985). *Technology's storytellers: Reweaving the human fabric.* Cambridge, Mass.: The Society for the history of Technology/MIT Press.

Stevick, E. W. (1990). *Humanism in language teaching: A critical perspective.* Oxford: Oxford University Press.

Strain, J. E. (1986). Method: Design-procedure versus method-technique. *System, 14*(3), 287-294.

Stronks, G. G., & Blomberg, D. (Eds.). (1993). *A vision with a task: Christian schooling for responsive discipleship.* Grand Rapids: Baker.

Stronks, J. K., & Stronks, G. G. (1999). *Christian teachers in public schools: A guide for teachers, administrators, and parents.* Grand Rapids: Baker.

Sullivan, J. (2000). *Catholic schools in contention: Competing metaphors and leadership implications.* Dublin: Veritas.

Taylor, W. (Ed.). (1984). *Metaphors of education.* London: Heinemann.

Thiessen, E. J. (1990). A defense of a distinctively Christian curriculum. In L. J. Francis & A. Thatcher (Eds.), *Christian perspectives for education* (pp. 83-92). Leominster: Gracewing.

Thiessen, E. J. (1997). Curriculum after Babel. In J. Shortt & T. Cooling (Eds.), *Agenda for Educational Change* (pp. 165-180). Leicester: Apollos.

Thiessen, E. J. (2001). *In defence of religious schools and colleges.* Montreal: McGill-Queen's University Press.

Thiselton, A. C. (1992). *New horizons in hermeneutics: The theory and practice of transforming biblical reading.* London: HarperCollins.

Thiselton, A. C. (1999). Communicative action and promise in interdisciplinary, biblical, and theological hermeneutics. In R. Lundin, C. Walhout and A. C. Thistleton (Eds.), *The promise of hermeneutics.* Grand Rapids: Eerdmans.

Thompson, T. R. (1998). Ungrasping ourselves: A kenotic model of multicultural encounter. In T. R. Thompson (Ed.), *The one in the many:*

Christian identity in a multicultural world (pp. 9-24). Lanham: University Press of America.

Thornbury, S. (1991). Metaphors we work by: EFL and its metaphors. *ELT Journal, 45*(3), 193-200.

Todorov, T. (1983). *The conquest of America* (R. Howard, Trans.) San Francisco: Harper & Row Publishers.

Tracy, D. (1979). Metaphor and religion: The test case of Christian texts. In S. Sacks (Ed.), *On Metaphor* (pp. 89-104). Chicago: University of Chicago Press.

Van Brummelen, H. (1992). Of dissonant rhapsody and harmonic fugue: The role of metaphor in the interplay of theory and practice in education. *Faculty Dialogue, 17*, 169-184.

Van Brummelen, H. (1994). *Stepping stones to curriculum: A biblical path.* Seattle: Alta Vista College Press.

Velten, D. (1995). Christian thinking in education. *Spectrum, 26*(1), 59-70.

Vryhof, S., Brouwer, J., Ulstein, S., & VanderArk, D. (1989). *12 affirmations: Reformed Christian schooling for the 21st century.* Grand Rapids: Baker.

Walsh, B. J. (1996). Reimaging biblical authority. *Christian Scholar's Review, 26*(2), 206-220.

Walsh, B. J. (2000). Transformation: Dynamic worldview or repressive ideology? *Journal of Education and Christian Belief, 4*(2), 101-114

Weeks, N. (1980). In defence of Christian schools. *Journal of Christian Education*(67), 21-29.

Weeks, N. (1988). *The Christian school: An introduction.* Edinburgh: Banner of Truth.

Wells, S. (1998). *Transforming fate into destiny: The theological ethics of Stanley Hauerwas.* Carlisle: Paternoster Press.

Wessels, A. (1994). *Europe: Was it ever really Christian?* London: SCM.

Wilder, A. N. (1983). Story and story-world. *Interpretation, 37*, 353-364.

Wilson, J. (1956). *Language and the pursuit of truth.* Cambridge: Cambridge University Press.

Wink, W. (1989). *Transforming Bible study*, 2nd ed. Nashville: Abingdon.

Wolters, A. M. (1985). *Creation regained: Biblical basics for a reformational worldview.* Grand Rapids: Eerdmans.

Wolters, A. M. (1989). On the idea of worldview and its relation to philosophy. In P. A. Marshall & S. Griffioen & R. J. Mouw (Eds.), *Stained glass: Worldviews and social science* (pp. 14-25). Lanham: University Press of America.

Wolterstorff, N. (1980). *Educating for responsible action.* Grand Rapids: Eerdmans.

Wolterstorff, N. (1981). Is reason enough? *Reformed Journal, 31,* 20-24.

Wolterstorff, N. (1982). Introduction. In H. Hart & J. Van Der Hoeven & N. Wolterstorff (Eds.), *Rationality in the Calvinian tradition.* Lanham: University Press of America.

Wolterstorff, N. (1984). *Reason within the bounds of religion* (2nd ed.). Grand Rapids: Eerdmans.

Wolterstorff, N. (1989). On Christian learning. In P. A. Marshall & S. Griffioen & R. J. Mouw (Eds.), *Stained glass: Worldviews and social science* (pp. 56-80). Lanham: University Press of America.

Wolterstorff, N. (1995). *Divine discourse: Philosophical reflections on the claim that God speaks.* Cambridge: Cambridge University Press.

Wolterstorff, N. (1997). Suffering, power, and privileged cognitive access: The revenge of the particular. In D. A. Hoekema & B. Fong (Eds.), *Christianity and culture in the crossfire* (pp. 79-94). Grand Rapids: Eerdmans.

Wolterstorff, N. (1999). Can scholarship and Christian conviction mix? A new look at the integration of knowledge. *Journal of Education and Christian Belief, 3*(1), 33-49.

Wright, N. T. (1991). How can the Bible be authoritative? *Vox Evangelica, 21,* 7-32.

Wright, N. T. (1992). *Bringing the church to the world.* Minneapolis: Bethany House.

Wright, N. T. (1992). *The New Testament and the people of God.* London: SPCK.

Wright, N. T. (1996). *Jesus and the victory of God.* London: SPCK.

Wynne Jones, R. (2000, 16 March 2000). Pimps and pushers were once my heroes. *The Express,* pp. 42-43.

Index